HER MIDDLE NAME IS COURAGE

How Self-Leadership Transforms Pressure into **Performance**, Chaos into **Clarity**, and Rage into **Resilience**

HEIDI DENING

A SPIRITCAST
NETWORK BOOK

First published in 2018 by Heidi Dening
Sydney, New South Wales, Australia

© Heidi Dening

The moral rights of the author have been asserted.
This book is a SpiritCast Network Book.
National Library of Australia Cataloguing-in-Publication data:

Author:

    Dening, Heidi

Title:

    Her Middle Name is Courage; How Self-Leadership Transforms Pressure into Performance, Chaos into Clarity, and Rage into Resilience.

ISBN:

    978-1-791-59112-0

Subjects:

    Leadership, Business, Self-Improvement, Motivation, Entrepreneurship

All rights reserved. Except as permitted under the Australian Copyright Act 1968 (for example, a fair dealing for the purposes of study, research, criticism or review), no part of this book may be reproduced, stored in a retrieval system, communicated or transmitted in any form or by any means without prior written permission. All enquiries should be made to the publisher at info@heididening.com

Editor-in-chief: Anita Saunders, Cherise Lily Nana
Cover Design: Bliss Inventive

Disclaimer:
The material in this publication is of the nature of general comment only, and does not represent professional advice. It is not intended to provide specific guidance for particular circumstances and it should not be relied on as the basis for any decision to take action or not take action on any matter which it covers. Readers should obtain professional advice where appropriate, before making any such decision. To the maximum extent permitted by law, the author and publisher disclaim all responsibility and liability to any person, arising directly or indirectly from any person taking or not taking action based on the information in this publication.

Dedication

This book is dedicated to the most gorgeous leprechaun
on the planet ... my husband.

Thank you for always making me giggle and inspiring me to find my
courage, even during my wobbliest of times.

You are the best pot of gold a gal could hope to find.

I love you more than you will ever know,
Heidi Jane xx

Praise for *Her Middle Name Is Courage* and Heidi Dening

This Book Is Captivating, Tangible, Compelling and a Glorious Gift to the World

"Gut wrenching, empowering, and thoroughly pragmatic. 'Her Middle Name is Courage' is an impossible to ignore, call to action, for anyone who wants to do more, be more, have more, and give more. Heidi Dening is indeed gutsy and this book will remind you how gutsy you can be. Having this depth of courage and this level of resilience is essential for leaders if they want to shine in their workplaces. For those who lack confidence or direction it is known that we often do our best reflection, decision-making and planning outside of office hours. This is a book that facilitates that development journey."

Cath Nolan, Gender Gap Gone

A Triumphant Story of Resilience

"Her Middle Name Is Courage' is an inspiring, yet practical book from an authentic leader who has risen from adversities and now shares her positive insights so we can all learn to step into our true potential. Heidi's stories of transformation and truth telling are relevant to everyone who is ready to find their own courage and be the great self-leader they are destined to be. Like the Phoenix, she has regenerated and resurrected to become an even more determined, resilient, inspiring, healthy, and regal woman than she was before. I love her teachings about the Resilience Bucket and can see how these strategies would make a huge impact on workplaces around the country."

Sarah Fisher, BigFish Consultancy

A Courageous Book by a Courageous Person

"Heidi has faced adversity that would leave most of us quivering in the corner asking for a cease-fire. Instead she has shown us through her actions, and now her words, how to build self-leadership and grow from the unwanted cruel lessons that chose to test her fortitude. Lucky for us, she is here, and sharing her techniques for not just surviving adversity but thriving because of it. This book is filled with wonderful stories and powerful lessons that individuals, teams and companies could learn from to transform their challenging situations into positive opportunities."

Guy Newman, Newmemory Australia

This is the Book that Just Might Change Your Life

We need a bigger word for courage when it comes to describing Heidi's stories that she so humbly shares here. The inspiration and clarity will come quickly. You will feel stronger, more self aware and ready to conquer, once you have immersed yourself in 'Her Middle Name is Courage.' There is no victim to be found, only wisdom and determination. They say we all have a book in us and it thrills me to know that Heidi typed hers out for us all to learn from. It's both validating and thought provoking to read, whilst providing a practical lens for those of us who want to learn more and be more. The insights, learnings and stories just kept on coming. Self-leadership is something we all need to have top of mind regardless of industry, role or position. Resilience is a life skill that changes who we are and how we lead in the world. And that's all covered here in one book! If you want to know who you are really capable of being, then this is the book for you. "

Lisa Stephenson, Lisa Stephenson Consulting

Everyone In My Life Needs To Read This Book

"Heidi Dening has written an utterly compelling masterpiece of a book in honesty, resilience, determination, authenticity and courage. I am blown away with the adversities she has endured, yet carries it all with such effortless grace. This book is outstanding - I want to shout it from the rooftops and buy a copy for everyone on the planet so we can make this world a better place."

Susan Watts, S J Consulting Group LLC.

Some Chapters Are Like The Gripping Movies We Yearn To Discover

"Reading 'Her Middle Name Is Courage' is a bit like catching up with an old friend, whilst at the same time learning from one of your most respected mentors. It's a book you want to settle in to, it keeps you interested so that you don't want to leave it, and some of the chapters are like the gripping movies we yearn to discover. It's a very moving book, I will be honest, I was brought to tears reading it on a number of occasions, but I also rejoiced in the inspiration and the learning to be gained from it. There are so many incredible insights to learn from, you almost want to start right back at the beginning again to read it all over just to make sure you fully take it all in. This book is so relevant for everyone at all levels, and it really needs to be shared!

Nikki Beaumont, Beaumont People.

Heidi Takes The Concept Of Self-Leadership To A Whole New Level.

"She talks to the courage that is in all of us, and she leads the way giving us ideas and inspiration to enlighten our own journeys. Heidi is a way-shower, a path-maker, and a light-bearer to stimulate all of us to keep our own journeys alive and kicking. She speaks from a lived experience that is authentic, compelling and loving. Read this book - it will be good for your soul."

Bill Carson, Inspire Learning

These Stories Are So Inspiring – What A Privilege To Read It

"It was perfect timing for me to gain inspiration from Heidi. Her ability to put things in perspective and provide the reader with real workable solutions is incredible. Heidi is a passionate and gifted author who reaches her readers in just the right way to inspire change. I thoroughly enjoyed reading Her Middle Name Is Courage."

Melony dos Remedios, Personal Training Academy.

Courageous by Definition

adjective; - not deterred by danger or pain; brave. This is the story of Heidi Dening…

"What an amazing story of resilience, persistence and determination. A true lesson book for any experienced or aspiring leader who wants to truly grow as a person, develop their emotional intelligence and live a life of fulfilment. Heidi highlights the absolute necessity for a leader to be able to self-reflect, focus on their strengths, dispel self-limiting beliefs and gain the guts to positively influence their own life first, in order to become a truly inspirational leader in every area of their life, in every relationship - Someone that can focus on the good in every situation and positively influence themselves as well as others.

This book is an essential read for every human wanting to find their true meaning and unleash their God-given potential, while here in this life…Truly inspirational!"

Jerry Kennard, Evoke Projects

A Life-Empowering Primer

"Her Middle Name is Courage is for anyone searching for a roadmap to create a more direct and powerful life-path. Heidi has faced adversity and hardship and seen her dreams explode quite literally at her feet, yet, she's managed to dust herself off, always ready for the next challenge. Her unfettered determination can teach us not only about refusing to succumb to adversity but also how to position ourselves as leaders to make a positive change."

Andrea Levin, Emmy Award Winning Writer and Producer

This Book Allows Us All To Be More Courageous and Become Better Individuals

"Heidi is a great communicator and inspires me through this book to look deep within myself and see what courage lies within. Through the challenges she has faced in life, she has been able to successfully self-reflect and use this as a catalyst to personal freedom and health. This in turn, helps us all to reflect and take on some of her learnings to be more courageous and better individuals."

Jamie Getgood, Getgood Consultancy

Contents

One
What Is Courageous Self-Leadership?
Page 1

Two
Who Can Be A Self-Leader?
Page 9

Three
Ordeal into Opportunity
Page 21

Four
Pressure into Performance
Page 35

Five
Disaster into Determination
Page 51

Six
Stupidity into Stability
Page 71

Seven
Setbacks into Self-care
Page 87

Eight
Chaos into Clarity
Page 101

Nine
The Resilience Bucket
Page 121

Ten
Rage into Resilience
Page 135

Eleven
Phoenix Rising
Page 157

What's Next?
Page 165

About the Author
Page 161

Gratitude
Page 167

Praise
Page 171

Message To My Readers

"Do not judge me by my success, judge me by how many times I fell down and got back up again."

Nelson Mandela

For many years, people have told me I should write a book about the real-life setbacks I have experienced and how I have been able to extract self-leadership strategies to ensure those experiences didn't break me.

Recently, it was the three-year anniversary of the night some men threw petrol bombs at my bedroom while I was overseas on a volunteer trip. Their intention was to burn me alive while I slept.

Writing this book (and that particular chapter called *Rage to Resilience*) has allowed me to finally draw something positive from that traumatic event that changed my life forever. In its aftermath, I could have succumbed to many more years of anxiety, hopelessness and gloom, but instead I eventually found the courage to accept what had happened and through small, incremental changes travel a new path to a stronger, happier and more fulfilled me.

I have now put onto these pages all the insights I have learned from rising above that harrowing incident. Just like the *Phoenix*, I have risen from the flames (literally) and overcome those difficult times. I talk more about this in the last chapter called *Phoenix Rising* followed by the programs and next steps that I developed to support myself with this transformation.

There is also three decades worth of other 'weird and wonderful' experiences from across the globe that have shaped my belief in the power of courageous self-leadership and after reading this book I hope you will be inspired to join me in embracing this for yourself.

It has turned my life around and I have now become a passionate advocate for introducing this concept to others, because I believe it is the resilient, optimistic self-leaders of this world who are making the biggest difference.

At the end of each chapter, you will find the positive insights that have been drawn from these stories of adversity and how I have turned them into easy-to-implement strategies. Even if you apply and share just one of them, collectively, the ripple effect could potentially influence the lives of hundreds of thousands of people. But first we need to motivate and influence ourselves.

This is not a leadership manual, a self-pity story, or a self-help book. It is a conversation with you about the learnings I've been able to extract from a series of adversities that I have experienced, how I've applied them to my life, and then utilised them to educate and inspire others to courageously flip adversity on its head and claim back their power.

There is no jargon, there are no fancy models, no references to scientific studies, and, no doubt, my grammar will not be perfect. I write how I speak, and I can't seem to do it any other way.

I believe we all have it in us to obtain gifts from the curve balls that life throws at us.

This book is your helping hand. It will help you to transform what has already gone on in your life into something positive, and help you become the authentic and gutsy self-leader that you are destined to be.

Her Middle Name Is Courage is not only for entrepreneurs, corporate executives, business owners, and team leaders. It's also for those who know they have so much more to offer but don't yet know how to turn their stories of adversity into acts of courage and reach their fullest potential both personally and professionally.

I hope the following stories and insights will fill you with inspiration and admiration, but mostly that they will light a fire of determination in your belly that will motivate you to step up, speak out, and share your brilliance in a way you haven't before. By digging deep and embracing the self-leadership strengths you already have, you too can leave your legacy by creating positive changes to our world.

Yours Courageously,

Heidi Dening x

Chapter One

What Is Courageous Self-Leadership?

> *The best people possess a feeling for beauty, the courage to take risks, the discipline to tell the truth, and the capacity for sacrifice.*
>
> Ernest Hemingway

There has not been a better time in history than now to build self-leadership skills. As a society, we have not only become disillusioned with the institutions that have historically commanded a lot of respect and confidence but we have also become disillusioned with the leaders who are in politics, sport, religion, entertainment, finance, the media, and our workplaces.

According to the annual Edelman Trust Barometer where tens of thousands of people from twenty-eight countries are surveyed, it's been revealed that the leading institutions in Australia, where I am from, are among the least trusted in the world. For the second year in a row, government, business, NGO's and the media all lost trust. Yes that's right, even our charitable organisations have lost the trust of more than half our population. It's crazy.

This lack of confidence in traditional leadership means we are less likely to believe everything we are told, we are more cynical than ever, and we are tired of being sold to and lied to. The amount of information and opinions we are bombarded with is overwhelming and it's hard to know who to have confidence in. When there are overnight 'influencers' who are often mistaken as 'leaders', it can be a case of style over substance, which causes us to lose connection with our own inner compass.

This is why it's more important than ever to develop our own self-leadership skills. The time has come to no longer look outwards for leadership, but rather to look within. To dig deep into our unique personal power and be galvanised to step up and shine.

Our world needs talented leaders.

Our workplaces need talented leaders.

But to be a talented leader you firstly need to be a talented self-leader.

And to be a talented self-leader, you need to have courage.

What Is Self-Leadership?

Self-leadership is having the ability and determination to influence yourself by habitually taking micro-steps and steering your life in a way that is right for you. It is not about sitting back and letting someone else shape how you are to evolve or where you are to end up. Positive outcomes will occur once you sit in the driver's seat of your life and draw on your confidence, motivation and capability to take the necessary actions to create change.

Not all of the time.

Not always in the way you intended.

Not always in the sequence you thought was important.

Not always knowing where it's going to lead you.

I've often felt a little like Dorothy from *The Wizard of Oz*. I am not sure what the Emerald City will look like at the end of the yellow brick road, but I know as long as I keep taking one more step forward, I will arrive at a wonderful destination.

Sometimes, this means taking three steps forward and five steps back, but with each step you build more confidence, you try more options, and odds are, you are more likely to reach better destinations.

Even if it is in a roundabout way.

I never would have thought that having petrol bombs thrown at my bedroom and waking up in a burning building could ever have built my confidence, given me more options in life, and led me to better destinations. It's taken three years since that event to understand that positive things can come out of such a trauma, but it's the truth.

This book is not a magic pill, or a shortcut method for you to go from where you are now to where you want to be. It is a book that will show you that through your adversities, through all the bumpy rides, through all the unjust, unfair, and undeserved setbacks, you can step up, speak out, and share the brilliance that is uniquely yours.

By being proactive in a world that continues to throw unexpected surprises, you can create a life that you are proud of, as long as you are realistic about the timeline, the effort needed, and the people you will need to support you along the way. Self-leadership is not about going it alone. It is about recognising what your strengths are, maximising them, and then acknowledging when you need to ask for help.

Self-Leaders Are The Definition Of Courage

Why?

Because they are paving their own path.

Because they are doing it their way.

Because they are learning from their own setbacks.

Because they are taking responsibility rather than blaming others.

Because they are courageously turning their own stories of adversity into stories of resilience.

Self-leaders understand that to be able to extract lessons and positivity from adversity, they firstly have to make sure their resilience buckets are full. I explain this powerful concept in chapter eight, *The Resilience Bucket*, but this starts with the repetition of small daily actions during the good times that can hold you together in times of struggle. The monotonous acts that are often hard, boring and relentless are what will support you when you need it most.

Acknowledging what must take priority takes a lot of self-awareness but it allows you to have clarity, direction and structure in your day, your week, and your life when things are not going to plan.

For example, when my Mum was dying, I had to be incredibly hard on myself to move my body every day, even when I had absolutely no time, and even when I would prefer to sit on the couch drinking wine instead. Being a carer for a loved one who is dying and is living forty-five minutes away is tough. When there are never-ending specialist appointments and dozens of emergency department visits, your life is not your own. When you are also running a thriving personal training business, with fifteen staff that opens at 6am and closes at 8.30pm, and you are the president of an international not-for-profit, and you are building a library on a remote island in another country, every second of your day is accounted for.

Movement though is the only thing that keeps me on track. I need to be obsessive about moving my body each day… even if that means just a gentle stretch in the morning in my lounge room. Because if I don't, then everything starts to unravel and since I am still responsible for my business, my staff and my customers, as a self-leader I recognise that I firstly need to be responsible for myself. And this starts with the daily action of moving my body. Every single day. Even when I have no time. Even when life seems out of control.

I am not going to give you a cookie-cutter program to follow because no doubt our lives are very different. We all have varying responsibilities, challenges, likes, dislikes and aspirations that are unique to our own lives.

What's good for me is not necessarily good for you.

What excites me does not necessarily excite you.

What challenges me does not necessarily challenge you.

The courage I need as a self-leader will be different to what you need. Comparing against each other is not advantageous because all adversities are relative to what has already been experienced.

This starts with the small daily habits that we put in place each and every day that can help us not be so reactive to stress, not be so reactive to adversity, and be able to rise above the challenges when they rear their ugly heads.

Because you see, we can't control what happens in our professional life. There will always be budget cuts, staff shortages, cash flow issues, impossible deadlines, annoying colleagues, and cranky customers.

And in our personal life there will likely be the loss of loved ones, injury, pain, ill health, small children, and ageing parents.

None of this we can control. All we have influence on is what we habitually put in place so we don't spiral out of control into burnout. Into depression. Into poverty. Into unemployment. Into loneliness. Into a place that is hard to come back from. Those good habits that bind us together in times of trouble, have to already be part of our everyday lives. This ensures that when life gets tough, when we are hit by that big curve-ball, then we have already built a strong, stable resilience bucket that allows us to shine ... rather than crumble.

The best sportsmen and women in the world teach us this lesson so well. Years before they are even close to winning a gold medal, a world cup, a grand slam or a big shiny trophy, they are habitually doing the mundane, boring, and repetitive work in the hope that it will someday allow them to maximise a once-in-a-lifetime opportunity. So when this opportunity finally comes, when the stress is really high and the pressure to win is off the chart, and everyone expects them to perform at their best, they are able to dig deep into their years of hard monotonous training and their years of sacrifices to enable them to give the best performance of their life.

This type of self-leadership starts with a belief that these small acts of dedication will lead somewhere positive but as we know, it requires courage to take that first step.

It takes courage to do this your way.

It is in our own stories, the good ones, the bad ones, the ones you hope you will never have to experience again, where we learn our life lessons. How we decide to respond to our adversities is what we will be remembered for and by embracing our tales of trepidation and triumphs we can rise above those who are still complacent and who are waiting for life / work / people to give them that extra edge.

We know, that it is those of us who are leading ourselves that will make the biggest impact in our workplaces, in our communities, and in our own courageous pathways.

I tip my hat to you for coming along with me, and joining this self-leadership movement.

Let's do this together.

Chapter Two

Who Can
Be
A Self-Leader?

> *"The most important battles that any leader has to face are resolved in that mysterious mental space we call the self."*
>
> Nigel Nicholson

Who Can Be A Self-Leader?

Everyone has the capability to develop the necessary skills to become a self-leader. Yes, that means you can too. I promise that no matter where you are right now in life, that you can turn your stories of struggle and transform them into stories of positivity. Believe me, I know personally when things are tough that this can feel out of your grasp, and that reasons such as fear, time, money and social status can get in the way of us truly believing in ourselves. If this happens, though, we end up living life with regrets as we watch it pass on by as we deal with that constant nagging feeling of living unfulfilled dreams and unexplored talents. None of us deserve this. It is such a shame to witness talented people make excuses and justify why they have 'missed out', knowing that with a little help, a little guidance, and a little courage they could flip adversity on it's head and claim back their power.

Self-leadership cannot be outsourced. This is a skill and a way of thinking and acting that you can only develop within yourself. No one can do it for you, and that is why self-leaders are so impressive and influential.

They can't fake it.

They can't steal it.

They can't pay for it.

The self-leaders of our world are authentic, resilient, and gutsy and are prepared to do whatever it takes to make a difference for themselves and for the greater good that they believe in.

A wonderful example of an impressive self-leader is Rosa Parks. She was a black seamstress in Alabama, USA, and in 1955 she refused to give up her seat for a white man despite what the segregation laws on buses demanded. Not only did Rosa display her deep belief in what is right and what is wrong, she also showed us that true self-leaders are courageous.

Over the years, Rosa also showed us how resilient you need to be when you decide to step up, speak out and show your brilliance. Rosa was arrested, she lost her job, and due to continual harassment and threats, she ended up having to move to another state. It didn't stop her though from continuing to fight for what she believed in and her persistence led to the US Supreme Court ruling that bus segregation was unconstitutional.

Rosa Parks became a nationally recognised symbol of dignity and strength in the struggle to end entrenched racial segregation.

This story is one example of many that proves that you don't need money, nor to be from the right social circle, to show self-leadership traits. All it takes is your willingness to dig deep into your own personal power, so your true potential can shine.

What Stops You From Becoming A Self-Leader?

Over the years I have worked with thousands of individuals, teams, and organisations and it amazes me how many people have lost confidence in their own abilities to shine their light.

There are so many talented, enthusiastic, inspiring individuals who are so close to becoming their best selves, but instead they get drowned in "justifications" that prevent them from stepping up and moving forward.

From the twenty-plus years that I have been doing what I do, here are the top five reasons I have heard from individuals as to why they don't step up to be the courageous self-leader they are capable of being.

1. "I can't be a self-leader because ... I don't have enough time."

There is no doubt that we all have a different perspective of time and what we can fit into our day, our week, our month, our year, and even our life.

There are periods when we all have extremely busy phases where it feels like we have no control over our schedules. Life is full of ebbs and flows and therefore it's important to acknowledge these phases and make the most of every minute whenever they become available to you.

This quote by Mandy Hale, a New York Times best-selling author and speaker, sums it up:

> *"Too busy" is a myth.*
> *People make time for the things that are really important to them.*

I definitely have fallen into the "I don't have time" hole over the years. In fact, often I really did have an incredibly full plate and it was nearly impossible to see a spare thirty seconds in my day. No doubt you can relate to this.

What I have come to realise though, is that, yes, sometimes there is no time to do anything extra without completely burning myself out, but I have also learnt when this is not the whole truth. On many other occasions, I am able to carve out some time for the activities I know I'm passionate about. The books that I know will inspire me. The courses that I know will challenge me. The people I know who will better me.

I think we can all agree that Bill Gates, the founder of Microsoft would have been (still is?) one of the busiest people on the planet and for this reason he is meticulous about the use of his time. Since becoming a billionaire, he often talks about the fact that he can buy whatever he wants, but he cannot buy more time. Therefore, one of his strategies is that he sets aside a specific amount of time to get a particular task done. For example, twenty minutes to answer five emails. Or one hour to write an article. This time management tool, called 'timeboxing' keeps you from getting distracted and ensures your productivity levels are kept high.

When we are striving to achieve something significant, being crystal clear about the end game helps us to feel okay about the sacrifices that need to be made along the way. By knowing your limits and rewarding yourself for small achievements, this will inspire you to make more time for the things you get rewarded for ... even when it is you rewarding yourself.

Set deadlines. This is really important to ensure you don't waste your precious time. Parkinson's Law tells us that work expands so as to fill the time available for its completion. In other words, if you don't put a cap on when you want to achieve it by, then the project could take forever.

Remember when you were at school and you were given an assignment that was due at the end of term? You would have eight to ten weeks to complete it, but if you were anything like me, you would wait till you had a week left and then get started. It didn't matter that you had the whole term because you kept convincing yourself that you had stacks of time left, then in that last week you worked like a machine around the clock to get that assignment in by the due date.

If you keep saying "now is not the time" or "I don't have the time" to do what you need to do to create a more abundant life, then you will be absolutely right about that. What you don't value does not get done. What you don't prioritise does not get done. But when you set a date, it can be surprising how you end up moving heaven and earth to get those big important rocks completed.

2. "I can't be a self-leader because ... I can't afford it."

We are not all born with a silver spoon in our mouth or a trust fund account or even a Plan B for when things go wrong. Many of us actually have to scrape and save and sacrifice to get ahead and become the person we want to be.

There is nearly always a way forward. Nearly always.

It's easy though to give up on the pursuit of where or who you want to be, with a "justification" such as, "I can't afford it." I can't afford a university degree. I can't afford an MBA. I can't afford to enrol in that leadership course.

So, what can you afford?

There are thousands of free online courses and educational podcasts that are on offer. When I was living with post-traumatic stress disorder, crippling insomnia, and constant pain for a year, I was not able to work. This obviously had a significant impact on my cash flow. I had always been used to earning enough money to do whatever I wanted, whenever I wanted. This was a new phase, and a phase I didn't much like.

Continual education has always been important to me, but due to no earnings, and my reduced physical and mental health, I wasn't able to enrol in the courses that I would normally be enticed by. Instead though, I found a whole range of free online ones that I could complete sitting safely at home, in my own time. Not all of them were fabulous, but most I learnt something from that allowed me to take one small step forward... which then gave me some purpose back into my life.

Can you enrol in an online course, learn something from it, and then apply this at work and get noticed? Can you find the courage to ask your manager if they would sponsor you for a full-day course that you have researched and know would help you to become a better employee? Then when you bring this knowledge back to your workplace, and prove that the return on investment has been worth their while, you can more confidently ask to be sent on a three-day course later in the year.

There are also many ways to earn extra money on the side – consider companies such as Airtasker, Upwork, Uber or Airbnb that might help you save the extra dollars to invest in yourself.

When Layne Beachley was number two in the world for surfing, she was working four different jobs and sixty hours a week. She had a dream, but that dream cost money and with only an $8000 a year sponsorship package, this meant she had to put in the hard yards herself. When one of her employers wrote her a cheque for $3000 so she could work less and train more it became a catalyst moment, and not only was she able to go on and achieve her goal which was to become a world champion, but she won that title seven times. What a legend.

Most of us know someone we could borrow a little money from. Yes, it is uncomfortable to ask, but if you approach them with a well-thought-out repayment plan you might be pleasantly surprised with their answer. Who knows, you could end up getting a pay rise and your debt could be repaid in half the agreed time.

If you want something bad enough, if you want to get ahead, if you want to become the self-leader you know you can be, there is always a way.

Be creative. Be tenacious. Be courageous. And make it happen.

3. *"I can't be a self-leader because … I've got children."*

There is no doubt that juggling children and work responsibilities takes extra effort, organisation, patience, and money.

The great thing is that it is also an extra driver.

An extra motivator.

What better way to bring up smart, self-reliant, savvy children than by walking your talk, being the role model you were cut out to be, and showing your children from a very early age that success in life (no matter how you define it) takes effort, takes persistence, and takes courage.

No one said this would be easy, but imagine the rewards of watching your children walk in your footsteps and deciding for themselves that they have their own special brilliance to share with the world and they have the confidence and courage to step up and speak out and shine their light.

No amount of money, nor pay rises, nor work perks would ever be more motivating than this.

Naomi Simpson, founding director of Red Balloon and a shark on the acclaimed TV show *Shark Tank* Australia says,

"The reason I started my business was because of my kids. What I want is resilient children, who are respectful and responsible ... My job is to give them their value set and their work ethic, so they can get a sense of accomplishment and achievement."

Her own mum had been a successful professional in the 1960s, which helped her to shape her own path.

"I remember watching Mum head off to work in her suit every morning and thinking to myself, 'Gee, that looks fabulous. When I grow up I want to be just like her.' I owe a lot to my Mum and the incredible example she set for me, and for keeping me on the right track."

4. "I can't be a self-leader because ... I haven't had big life challenges to learn from."

There is a lot of hype about having to endure hardships before you can learn any worthwhile life lessons. There is no denying that tough times actually do teach us something, but the reality is that many people learn self-leadership lessons from reading books like this one, or being mentored or educated in their workplace. Others learn self-leadership from watching interviews about those who have had adversity and what they have learnt. In the case of Leigh Sales, the ABC TV host on the *7.30pm Report*, she learnt worthwhile life lessons from actually conducting the interviews herself. Up until recently, she confesses that she led a charmed life, but I'm sure you would agree, that she always displayed great self-leadership qualities ... many of them, no doubt, gained from the thousands of people she has interviewed.

As you are about to read, I have had some fairly unique, often extreme events in my life. These events have led me to write this book. The thing is, you do not need to have unusual or intense or life-threatening incidents to prove you have great self-leadership skills.

All you need is to be shown how to extract lessons from your own stories - big ones and small ones - so you are ready and prepared for when they are needed.

5 *"I can't be a self-leader because ... I'm not from the right background, school, suburb or social circle."*

I'll never forget one night when I was out with a college friend and meeting her friends from high school for the first time. They had all gone to expensive private schools and lived in beautiful big homes in very upmarket parts of Sydney. When they asked me where I lived (suburb in the north west of Sydney) and what school I went to (the local high school), I could see them actually repel from me. In their minds, I did not have the background, connections, upbringing, or education to make me worthwhile talking to.

This attitude still exists amongst sectors of society all around the world. We cannot avoid it, hide from it, or even have much control of it.

What we don't want is for it to stop us from moving forward and taking those micro-steps that will help us to create the professional (and personal) life that we deserve.

A great example of someone who did not let her circumstances stop her from becoming a confident self-leader is Malala Yousafzai. Malala was the young fifteen-year-old girl from the north of Pakistan who was shot in the face by the Taliban because she was fighting for her right as a female to be educated. Despite not being from the 'right' background, school, suburb, gender or social circle, Malala not only survived this horrific crime, she went on to become the youngest ever winner of the Nobel Peace Prize, and has continued with her plight to champion universal access to education. She is the epitome of a courageous self-leader.

Like Malala, I have no shame about where I was brought up or where I went to school. I feel proud that I have curated my life in the way that I have, despite what those snooty rich kids thought of me. In fact, I feel so bloody privileged to have been brought up with parents who loved me deeply, who worked incredibly hard to give me every opportunity possible, and who gave me the trust in myself to take all my micro-steps.

I understand that not everyone has been as lucky as me because not everyone gets to grow up with loving support and encouragement. The reality is that we can't change what we can't change. Being a self-leader does not happen because you were born into wealth, or you had a family business to walk into, or you were handed the best education on a platter.

No.

Self-leadership is a trait that you can acquire by being determined to positively influence your own life.

Self-leaders are authentic, resilient, and gutsy, and they willingly step up to the challenges of this uncertain, complex, and ever-changing world that we live in … even when it would feel far simpler to remain the same.

Albert Einstein has been credited for saying, ***"The definition of insanity is doing the same thing over and over again and expecting a different result."***

The first step to becoming a courageous self-leader is to proactively decide that you are no longer going to do the same thing over and over, you have had enough of the status quo, and that you do not want everything to remain the same for one more minute. You have to truly believe that there is no more time to waste, no more life to waste, and no more opportunities to waste.

The following chapters of this book are a mix of unique stories and self-leadership insights. The purpose is to highlight the potential of courageously turning stories of adversities into stories of positivity and how these insights can propel our personal and professional lives to great heights. I hope you enjoy reading them as much as I have enjoyed writing them.

Chapter Three

Ordeal into OPPORTUNITY

> "*If opportunity doesn't knock, build a door.*"
>
> Milton Berle

One morning, when I was eleven years of age, I woke up unable to walk.

I will never forget that feeling of knowing that if I tried to get out of bed, I would fall in a heap on the floor because I actually knew that my legs no longer worked. I called out for my Mum and when I told her, I think she thought I was sleep-talking because she just said to close my eyes, and that when I woke up again everything would be fine. She was my Mum, and she did know best, so I did what I was told.

Unfortunately, though, mother nature decided that my bladder was so full that it couldn't wait any longer. I tried to get up as my Mum's words resonated in my ears – it was probably only a dream (or a nightmare) – but bang, I fell flat on my face onto the floor.

OMG ... I couldn't believe it. I really could not walk. I screamed out for Mum and Dad who came charging into my room thinking my room must be on fire for me to have belted out such a blood-curdling noise. Mum stood there in shock in her pyjamas looking at me in disbelief lying in a heap on the floor, while Dad raced around searching for the cause of my scream. Had someone broken in and hurt me?

Mum, being the gentle soul, knelt down beside me and tried to calm my fears, while Dad hoped that I was playing a trick and said, *"Come on Heidi Jane, stop fooling around."* Once they both realised that I actually could not get up, I could see the panic in their eyes and my bottom lip started to wobble. I felt incredibly vulnerable lying there on the floor in my Mum's arms while she unsuccessfully tried to tell me that it would all be okay. The look on her face told a very different story.

It's amazing in situations like this how our minds race straight to the insignificant things we will not be able to do that day, that week. I clearly remember thinking about how I had only recently been named top female sports star of the year at my primary school - a title that I was incredibly proud of. In a month, I was going off to represent my school in my zone carnival in numerous track and field events, plus Dad and I had our annual City-to-Surf race to run in together. These events were soooooo important to me and I had no time or tolerance for legs that didn't work.

That first morning of disbelief and panic, became eight months of hardship and uncertainty. On good days I used a walking frame to get around, but on bad days when Dad was not there to hoist me over his shoulder, the best I could manage was to drag myself with my arms along the floor. Everything was such an ordeal and took such a long time and I wondered if I was going to always be looking at people's feet… rather than their faces.

I saw half a dozen different specialists in that first four months. A couple of them told me that I was making it all up and it was all in my head, but the most common diagnosis was that I had caught a strange virus that had attacked my nerves and all we could do was hope that eventually it might run its course. The reality was that no one knew what to do because they really couldn't put their finger on what was wrong.

This meant that they couldn't give me antibiotics so it would go away. They couldn't give me a series of injections that would spark my muscles to move again. They couldn't send me to the latest treatment centre where I would get round-the-clock help.

Learning:
A quick-fix is not always available,
especially when you need it most.

I was afraid that I would never walk again, I was embarrassed that Dad would have to carry me over his shoulder everywhere, and I was angry because some of the doctors would look at me as if it was my fault, and would tell me to "get up and walk." By the way, my Dad did not take lightly to this attitude from them, and it took every little bit of restraint for him not to scream at them and say, *"Hey that's my number one daughter you are doubting, something is terribly wrong, fix her or I will…"*

I missed a lot of school that year and in the end the doctors said there was a seventy-five percent chance I would never walk unassisted again. I was so scared, but when one night I overheard Dad whispering and Mum crying in our lounge room about the fact I might end up in a wheelchair, I became petrified.

For those tumultuous eight months of my life, I lost a lot of confidence in my physical abilities, and due to being home for so long I also lost confidence in myself. I was often too embarrassed to go out in public because everyone would stare, and little kids would point and laugh at me. I couldn't believe I had gone from being little Miss Sporty Spice, to little Miss Why-Is-She-So Weird Spice.

When you are eleven, about to go into high school, and are used to spending all of your spare time running, playing tennis, doing gymnastics, and riding your bike, it's a big ordeal to be so dependent, housebound and ridiculed. There were times when I would cry and cry, thinking I would never be able to walk again and that no one would want to be my friend because I "walked" like such a weirdo.

As those days turned into weeks, and those weeks turned into months I made a decision that this was not going to be my life. I had always been strong-minded but now I had determination mixed with desperation. By this stage ... six months of not being able to use my legs properly... I was sick of staring at people's feet.

It's not until you have an injury, a virus, or an accident that you realise the harsh reality of the recovery process. That single moment when you fall off your bike or twist your knee at netball, or you get hit by a car, can bring months, if not years, of boring, relentless and often painful rehabilitation.

One of the few doctors who took me seriously, set me a program of exercises and this gave me my first glimmer of hope. To my eleven-year-old mind this was like being lost in a cave with only the one naked flame (this new exercise program) to comfort me and direct me towards my escape. I was going to do everything in my power to ensure this flame led me to my recovery.

So with gritty determination I fought this strange, unknown virus in my body with everything I could.

Learning:
Self-leaders - even at an early age - have the mental strength and determination to strive onwards and upwards.

I started to get a fire in my belly and applied every bit of willpower I could muster and imagine myself doing all the things in life that I wanted to do. As a young little girl who is dragging herself across the floor, picturing her life ahead, this was not a long list. I was going to run again with my Dad, play tennis with my team, ride my bike with the other Werona Street warriors (a bunch of kids my age on my street), and roller-skate with my boy crush at the time, Geoffrey – even though Dad had other ideas about that part.

Whenever Mum and Dad counted out the repetitions of my rehabilitation exercises, usually in sets of ten, I pushed it to eleven or twelve. I was definitely afraid that the program wouldn't work but I was also very resolute - failure was not an option.

It was a slow rehabilitation process that was boring, relentless, and often painful as I stretched my limits further every session. I was impatient and felt that I had wasted enough time feeling sorry for myself, and was more than ready to be better, stronger, fitter, and more fabulous than ever before. Each micro-step I took (physically and mentally) got me closer to my goal, and after eight long months of the unknown I no longer needed my flame (or my frame) as I had made it out of that dark cave and I regained full control of my legs. Yah ☺

And can I tell you that those legs have gone on to do some amazing things.

Before I write about that though, I have to say that this is why adversity can be so positive, because when you come out of it, overcome it, recover from it, and beat it, you know how lucky you are.

Ordeal into OPPORTUNITY

In the whole scheme of life, eight months isn't a long time to be incapacitated compared to people who suffer with lifelong disabilities, and this experience certainly gave me an insight and empathy for the challenges that they encounter every single day. This helped me to become aware of just how lucky I am. I am now able to physically do whatever I want to do, and I never take this for granted.

Those legs that could not even get my body to the bathroom ended up running thousands of kilometres over the years. I have run in probably fifty fun runs that ranged from eight to fourteen kilometres; two half-marathons; ten international running relays; an Olympic-length triathlon; and my greatest athletic achievement of all, a full forty-two-kilometre Olympic marathon.

In fact, this particular marathon was in Sydney in 2001. We followed the blue line that the world's best marathon runners had taken during the Sydney Olympics Marathon event the previous year. We started in North Sydney, went across the Harbour Bridge, around the Opera House, through the Botanical Gardens, across the Anzac Bridge, and out to the Olympic Stadium.

Those elite Olympians had completed the exact same route, along that exact same blue line only twelve months before. When I crossed that finish line, physically and mentally exhausted, I curled into a ball on the ground in the middle of the stadium and sobbed, as I felt completely overwhelmed with this achievement, knowing what I had gone through to accomplish it. It was a once-in-a-lifetime opportunity and I felt privileged that these legs were able to do this for me.

I have often reflected back to the time when I couldn't walk. Of how if we had listened to the first specialist we saw that I may have given up on my capacity to heal. Mum wouldn't back down though until she found someone who was really listening to what I was experiencing. I witnessed this "don't give up" attitude of Mum's so many times during my life, and I am sure her continual role modelling of this attitude (especially through her own times of adversity) has helped shape a similar belief that I have applied to my own life.

My Dad was the same. When he died, we found in his wallet a little piece of paper with the following written on it:

> ***"Losing is not coming second.***
> ***Losing is knowing you haven't done your best.***
> ***I have never lost."***

I love this attitude to life, and on reflection, when I think back to that ordeal of not being able to walk, and how I applied sheer determination, sweat, blood, and tears to my rehabilitation, it was because of this belief that my parents had unconsciously instilled in me from an early age.

The fact was, I might not have walked unassisted again, but I was damn well going to try hard to ensure I could. I was going to give it my very best efforts because this was the least I could do for myself. These strong attitudes that my parents instilled in me have evolved into a personal motto that I have embraced for decades, and that is ***"If it's going to be, it's up to me."***

Back when I was eleven I knew somehow that if I wanted to walk, jump, skip, and play tennis again, I would need to be the one to make that happen. If it was going to be, it was going to have to be up to me. The opportunities that have come to me because of applying this motto have been and will continue to be great.

Self-leadership is what got me through that ordeal - way before I understood that self-leadership was a thing.

In a workplace, there are many ordeals that get thrown your way. The key is finding tactics to turn those ordeals into opportunities. And that takes courage because it is easy to say that things haven't turned out the way you want for this reason or that reason and then give up. For example, if a colleague who does not have the experience or know-how gets promoted into a position that you have applied for, it's hard to see it as an opportunity. If you believe you have put the hard yards in over and above the call of duty, this makes no sense. When you have shown dedication and loyalty and stuck with the company through all its financial, staffing, and technical challenges, this does not seem right. When you have listened to your managers whinge about their circumstances, their ordeals, yet they choose someone else, it does not seem fair.

When the workplace is unfair and doesn't make sense, what can you do? How can you turn this into an opportunity?

Firstly, you need to get all of the emotions out of your system so you can move forward into the next step, which is the decision-making process. If you stay bitter and twisted, and let your emotions, "what ifs", and swearing circle around in your head, it will hold you back. Get comfortable with the facts, face the reality, and get crystal clear clarity on what is the most impactful micro-step that you can take next.

To do this you need to gather all the information, evaluate the positives and negatives, talk it through with a trusted advisor, and then confidently turn the ordeal into your next opportunity.

I know this is easier said than done, but there is no point wallowing in self-pity for too long. Take it from me – no one really listens. Ha ha. Because you see, life is filled with opportunities, even when the ordeals feel like they are drowning you.

Having people who believe in you makes such a difference. When my legs stopped working, if it wasn't for my Mum's comforting arms and never-ending love, plus my Dad's strong shoulders and that glint of pride that lit up his eyes whenever I pushed for one more repetition or for a few extra wobbly steps, I could not have done it. They were always that positive flame encouraging me and supporting me out of dark caves, and now that they are gone, I miss them so so much.

Reflection

This ordeal of not being able to walk taught me self-leadership strategies on how to never take no for an answer, how to be grateful for good health, and how to embrace every opportunity that comes my way.

What are the ordeals you've already experienced in your life?

How have they influenced you?

What have you learnt from them?

How have you transformed them into opportunities?

I learnt the following *Self-Leadership Strategies* from my Inability to Walk ORDEAL

1. Never Take No For An Answer

Even experts don't always know everything. When you have to navigate yourself through the medical world, this becomes pretty apparent.

The business world is also full of self-proclaimed "experts" who believe that they have all the right answers. There are narcissists in our workplaces, overnight 'influencers' in the media, and specialists who convince us they are like super heroes.

When something doesn't sit right with you though, don't ignore it or be silenced by it. If you feel your internal compass is off track, look deeper into why this is so. Question it, unpack it, and sift through it until you understand it fully.

If you are told you are not good enough, smart enough, tall enough, qualified enough, keep on trying. Don't take no for an answer if it is something you believe in.

Self-leaders will continually focus on what they believe is the truth and work hard until they get what they know is right for themselves and their teams.

2. The Gift of Good Health

I love to move and therefore when I am injured or unwell it has a negative impact on all parts of my life. It impacts my confidence, my mental health (especially my ability to deal with stress), my ability to create specific education programs for organisations, my ability to get more done in less time with fewer mistakes, my ability to lead my team, my ability to fall asleep and stay asleep, my self-esteem, plus my husband will tell you it also impacts my ability to be a happy, friendly person!

Movement has become a crucial component of my daily life and if I had not recovered, I am unsure how I would have coped in many situations over the upcoming decades.

Of course, many people around the world have 'same same but different' circumstances, where one day life is perfectly normal and then the next everything has changed. When you have experienced the fragile tightrope of life, you take a very different view of it.

This is why our workplaces must understand their important role in maintaining (or improving) the health and wellbeing of their people, because having physically and mentally strong employees puts you in the fast lane to business success.

Since we spend 90,000 hours of our lives at work, it cannot be a place that puts our wellbeing at jeopardy. Companies must put their number one asset - their people - first.

They need to create environments that allow individuals to thrive so they can be productive, creative, analytical, strategic, and focused. So they can enthusiastically collaborate with others in their team and produce results that impact the overall success of the organisation.

The companies I see doing this best are ones that adopt flexible work policies and provide relevant education programs, so that everyone can prioritise and embrace the gift of good health.

3. OPPORTUNITIES

Opportunities do reveal themselves in many different ways. We just have to make sure we have the right glasses on so that we see them in all their brilliance. When we are bogged down in life, worrying about insignificant issues, sweating the small stuff, it is like we walk around with blinkers on. We see everything in black or white.

Self-leaders see the world as a rainbow or as a degustation meal. They are aware of the many options to pick and choose from, but they also have the wisdom to know that those opportunities may not always be available.

When life is going your way, you take it for granted that you will always have it good. This makes it easy to pass up opportunities because you think you'll have all the time in the world to seize them. The reality is that this may not always be the case.

At work, it is easy to stick with the status quo. To go with the flow. To stay within your comfort zone. For self-leaders though, staying comfortable can be like living a vanilla life. They want to make sure they get to taste all the flavours so they can make the most of what this incredible world has to offer.

Embracing opportunities that come your way and leaning in to the uncomfortable will allow you to experience a full life in all its brilliance.

Closing Chapter Reminder

Ordeals can be transformed into opportunities once we draw on the positive insights gained from our adversities.

When we courageously embrace the powers of self-leadership and habitually take action in a way that is right for our lives, we can step up and create real and sustainable change.

Over time this means that together, as resilient, optimistic and inspired self-leaders we can make the most impactful difference to our lives, to our workplaces, to our communities, and to our world.

Chapter Four

Pressure into PERFORMANCE

*"Continuous effort,
not strength nor intelligence,
is the key to unlocking our potential."*

Winston Churchill

As I was growing up, apart from wanting to be just like Wonder Woman (athletic, smart and with super powers), all I dreamt of was becoming a Physical Education and Health teacher. Due to being such a sporty spice from an early age, there was nothing else that even came close and there was no doubt in my mind that I would accomplish it.

Unfortunately, though, I hit my first hurdle on the road to my dream career, thanks to the so-called experienced advice of my careers advisor.

In Year 10, we had a special day dedicated to learning about life after high school and a personalised coaching session with our careers advisor. I was obviously still a naive fifteen-year-old but I actually felt proud to have a vocation goal, as most of my friends had no idea.

I can still see his pokey old office; the disorganised shelves, the badly fitting suit and this person of 'power' sitting behind a battered old desk who should have helped me make my dreams come true. When I think back now to that particular day I still feel angry, because that 'expert' careers advisor practically pulled my dream out from under me.

I remember how I enthusiastically explained to this so-called dream-maker of how I was going to be the best P.E. teacher ever. He looked at me with boredom while he checked his watch and thought about how long it was until lunch and told me in his dry monotone voice that the chances of me becoming a P.E. teacher were pretty low. He said I should give up on my dream and think about leaving school because a secretarial TAFE course would be far better suited to my abilities.

What? You're joking, aren't you? It was like I had been hit in the stomach and all the air had been sucked from my lungs and I couldn't get any more in. I could not believe what I was hearing and managed to stutter out some questions about why he would say such a thing.

Looking again at his watch to see if it was any closer to lunchtime he simply said, *"Your current exam results are too low,"* and before I knew it I was outside his door, with my dream shattered. I could not believe it. What could I do? A secretary. I had never ever considered that I would have a desk job, I didn't really know anything about being a secretary - plus I didn't even know how to bloody type.

For the rest of that afternoon I was in a daze. I was absolutely devastated about this advice as I had grown up in a household where I had always been encouraged to strive for my goals and was made to believe that I could accomplish anything I set my mind to.

Apparently, I went missing that afternoon. I was due home at the normal 3.30 pm time, but I didn't get back till after 6 pm. Mum opened the front door and went from an angry look of *"where the hell have you been",* to a look of worry and concern as she could see from my eyes that I had been crying. I loved how my Mum's look of wrath could change so quickly because all she wanted to do was protect me from the world. You see, my eyes were so swollen from all the tears that I could hardly see out of them.

I have no memory of where I went that afternoon or what I did. I gather that I found a little corner somewhere and sobbed, as this "experts" advice sunk in.

That night I cried myself to sleep with words from the destroyer of dreams spinning around in my head. "Not good enough". "Leave school". "Become a secretary."

Why wouldn't I be able to achieve my goals?

Why didn't he believe in me?

Am I delusional about what I can achieve?

Am I that stupid that I should not even bother trying?

For the next three or four days I kept asking myself these questions. I was like that annoying child that continually asks why, only to be dissatisfied with the answer and then ask why again.

Was I disheartened? Damn right I was.

Was I devastated that my dream of standing up in front of a class being an inspiring P.E. and Health teacher had been shattered? Damn right I was.

Was I going to accept this so-called expert advice? Damn right I was NOT.

I knew if this was my dream then I was not going to let anybody take that away from me without me giving it my all. As I had learnt as an eleven-year-old with dodgy legs, if it's going to be, it's up to me.

Was I a great student at school? No not really, but that was more to do with the fact that I didn't push myself. Did I have the brains to get the exam results necessary? Yes, but only if I applied myself and there was no way I was going to let my career dream disappear due to a lack of trying.

So I set out on my road of determination, stubbornness, and my "I am going to prove you wrong" attitude, with such zest that I even surprised myself. I was not going to leave school. I was not going to do a secretarial course at TAFE. I was going to succeed.

Now I could sit here and pretend that I suddenly found all these new brain cells and it was easy. But it was not. I knew I had to work very hard during the remainder of my high school years if I was going to achieve my goal.

When it finally came to the Higher School Certificate (HSC) year though, all those feelings of doubt, insecurity and pressure reared their ugly head. What that career advisor had told me came flooding back and would not leave me. I wondered why on earth I hadn't taken his advice and left school as suggested because he obviously knew best … that I didn't have "the goods."

About March of that HSC year I developed an itchy rash all over my body. OMG, I am not sure if you have ever been really, really itchy for days, weeks, or months on end, but you feel like you are going insane. It is horrendous.

We tried so many pills and potions to alleviate the itch, but nothing worked. One day I ended up in the Emergency Department because the itch had got so bad that I was bleeding from scratching and I felt like I was losing the plot.

One specialist put it down to the stress and pressure I had put on myself about sitting my HSC exams and achieving my dreams. He told me it was my body's way of showing how stressed out it was feeling. I was glad that there was a reason for this dreadful itch but the big issue was that I still had to do my exams, and they were six months away. Oh noooooooo.

I suffered with that itch every minute of the day and night, and by the time it came to sit my exams, I was a walking wreck. My body looked like a leper with scabs and sores all over it, and my eyes were hanging out of my head as I hadn't slept properly for weeks ... months.

During the actual HSC I was given special allowances so that every hour I could go into the bathrooms with one of the supervisors and they would rub calamine lotion all over me to calm the itching. It is pretty hard to concentrate and focus when you are that uncomfortable and of course my catastrophising about how stupid I was did not help.

What is so interesting though, is that when I walked out of that last exam, within a few hours my itch stopped. Yep. No longer did I need to scratch. It was remarkable. I had worked myself into such a stressed-out state about getting enough marks to become a P.E. and Health teacher that my body's response had been to create this extreme reaction.

Learning:
The mind is powerful over the body so stay alert to the messages your brain is giving you.

So, what happened with my results? After all my stress, after the destroyer of dreams saying I wasn't good enough, I surprised everyone with my results, and went on to complete my Bachelor of Education (Personal Development/Health/Physical Education) and then a Graduate Diploma in Education.

The first door I wanted to bang on was that career advisor's to show him what I had completed, and say, *"Ha, I am better than what you thought."* But I didn't, and if the truth be known, due to that man's lack of insight into my abilities, that fire of determination in my belly may not ever have been lit.

Teaching P.E. and Health was everything I had hoped it to be apart from the challenging school I was originally sent to straight out of college. I have taught in fabulous schools here in Sydney, London, and Vanuatu and it was incredibly fulfilling to watch my students transform from being uncertain Year 7 girls into confident Year 12 young women.

Teaching taught me amazing skills - time management, public speaking, program development, strategic planning, and resilience (you try influencing up to two hundred teenage girls in a day who are hormonal cocktails – ha ha). Although I didn't stay as a secondary education teacher forever, I have continued to be an educator in some shape or form ever since, because I really believe in the truth and power of this saying...

> ***"If you give a person a fish, you feed them for a day.***
> ***If you teach a person to fish, you feed them for a lifetime."***

Education is where the magic happens. It is where life opportunities blossom.

The education skills that I originally gained have meant that I have now taught pimply teenagers to nourish their bodies; young children on a remote island in the Pacific to read; unhealthy adults to move more; stressed-out professionals to rejuvenate regularly; business leaders to create thriving work cultures; and entrepreneurs to embrace self-leadership strategies.

I haven't fed them for a day. I have fed them for a lifetime.

Because once you gain education, you can take the necessary micro-steps to get closer to your dreams. Whatever those dreams might be. Education unlocks potential and gives you the access key to bigger, brighter and better destinations.

The pressure that career advisor put on me was definitely unfair, but in fact it put a fire in my belly and a focus in my brain to ensure I could prove him wrong.

Learning:
Self-leaders are motivated by challenges.

By gaining my Education degree, opportunities were created for me to perform in a way that I never thought possible. After graduation, I was offered a P.E. position in a western suburbs school. Of course I said, "yes" because that is all I ever wanted to do. Nothing could have prepared me for what was to come though as it was not at all what I had imagined being a teacher would involve.

There were so many incidents that I could tell you about, but this particular incident was the straw that broke the camel's back. One night at about 10pm when I was driving some of my Year 9 dance group girls home from a concert that they had performed at, they asked to stop at a fast-food joint. I conceded due to them having been so well behaved all night and dancing their little hearts out.

As we drove through the drive-through, three Year 11 boys from our school approached the front of my car and started bouncing the bonnet up and down so it was smashing into the ground… for fun. I was petrified. Here I was with four fifteen-year-olds in my car, late at night, in a rough part of Sydney, and these big blokes were actually attacking us. I screamed for them to get away and finally they got bored and left us … we were all shaking.

The next morning I went straight to the principal to report them, as of course I knew who they were - they were on the basketball team. The principal listened intently but then told me that I was over-reacting and that "boys will be boys" and to just let it go. I had really thought they would have at least been suspended, so when I was politely dismissed from his office it was a real shock.

Learning:
Not all people who are given leadership positions are right for the job.

I think it was in that moment that I knew I would not stay at this school, and had to find myself a Plan B. If they could not support me in this type of situation, then I could not remain. It had been really frightening and to this day I am flabbergasted that those young men were not disciplined.

It's a good example though of choosing to do what is right for oneself. To digging deep and finding the courage to say, "this is not right." If my workplace does not value my personal safety, then it is not a place I want to be in.

And personal safety takes on many forms in a workplace. Since we spend decades of our lives at work, it is crucial that our physical and mental health is prioritised. In fact, Google ranks psychological safety as one of the top five dynamics that set their successful teams apart from their other teams.

I didn't know this at the time, but by saying "no" to a workplace that was not prepared to value my safety, I was demonstrating the first inkling of my professional self-leadership skills. And by saying "no," I opened up a whole new life trajectory. This workplace situation gave me an opportunity to step up, take some risks and create a new path which would lead to bigger and better things. So despite the fact that society puts alot of pressure on us to stay employed no matter what the circumstances, I fearlessly resigned and bought a one-way ticket to Europe.

When I finally returned to Australia after two and a half years of travelling around the world, I went back to teaching for a short while but the fact was my courage muscle had grown so much that I started to imagine bigger stages for my life performances.

I wanted more from my life, and although I loved teaching, my pay packet did not support my growing love of pretty dresses (with matching shoes!), but being an educator comes in many forms, and this new chapter of my life as an educator was about to begin.

I signed up for a course to become a personal trainer with the sole purpose of earning a little money on the side. I had no idea how much I was going to love educating adults (who would pay me money) on how to move more, nourish their bodies, and get the most out of life. After coming first in my class, I immersed myself in this new world.

When I started my new business called *Jump Start Your Life* out of my stinky garage with two hundred dollars' worth of second-hand equipment from Cash Converters, I really had no idea where it was going to lead me.

Learning:
Sometimes self-leaders don't even realise how courageous they are being until much later.

What started as a part-time business so I could buy some extra dresses developed into becoming one of the most successful personal training businesses of its type in Australia.

I grew a large talented team of trainers and support staff; I was asked to speak at conferences around the country and overseas to other up-and-coming personal trainers and fitness business owners; I won awards; and best of all we transformed the lives of thousands of local and global clients through easy-to-understand movement, nutrition, and rejuvenation education.

Jump Start Your Life became one of the best in Australia, it made millions of dollars, and I was able to sell it for the price and terms I asked for seventeen years later. In the end I had two couples that were prepared to commit to all my terms, and I got to choose. Incredible. Sort of. I mean, I had worked my butt off for seventeen years building a business that people aspired to owning, and really, when it comes down to it, I deserved that success. It's a funny thing to learn about yourself, that you have become a success in so many people's eyes.

I often wonder what came of that "careers expert" from my high school. What has he made of his life? What would he think if he found out that I had gone from what he considered to be an education dropout to someone who has received an Australia Day Merit Award for her education service? Ha.

And what would he think if he knew that the high school that he said I should leave because I had no hope of doing well had asked me back twenty-seven years later to be the keynote speaker at their end-of-year presentation night? The school's leadership team felt that my career was so inspiring that they wanted me back so I could motivate the current students to step up and do great things.

The irony of this was not lost on me.

Who would have thought that that young seventeen-year-old with an itchy rash all over her body because of the pressure she felt, could perform so well and turn her life into one that people admired. Not me.

That presentation night made me realise how much courage I had had over the years to step up and speak out and do what was right for me so I could thrive in all my pursuits.

As I prepared my speech for that night, I remembered that my high school path to success had actually not been that rosy. In fact, I had been caught smoking in the girls' toilets in year seven, was grounded from July – December in Year 9 due to my terrible half-yearly report, and there had been numerous other incidents that perhaps would indicate that I probably would not go on to performing that well in life.

The question I had during my speech preparation was whether or not there was any purpose in telling this side of me? How would this story benefit the audience or would it make me look like a loser? Should I just tell the inspiring parts of my story?

I decided at the last minute while I was on stage that I should tell this. The reasons being:

1. It was my story. This is who I am. That is who I was. Being truthful and authentic will always be a guiding value of mine.
2. I hoped that it gave all the parents sitting in the audience some hope that if they were trying to deal with their wayward teenagers, and wondering if it's possible for their kids to become something more than the rebellious, sarcastic, unengaged adolescents that they currently were, then I was the living, breathing, walking proof that a girl can go from being a pain-in-the-you-know-what to actually doing okay.
3. I also hoped that it would give the students in the audience who perhaps were still unsure of what direction life would take them or unclear on their life path that that is okay.
4. And finally, that if they had been told that they do not have what it takes to reach their dreams, to ignore that advice. All of us can achieve what we prioritise, and as long as we take ownership of our own life's path and keep taking micro-steps forward, then we will reach that destination.

To wrap that night up, I said, *"Sometimes when you are in high school it is hard to know where the yellow brick road can lead you, but that's not to say that it's not going to take you to great places ... or maybe to small places where you make a great difference. Listen to your body, recognise your strengths, get to know your passion, take note when your light goes on, and follow that feeling until it leads you somewhere worthwhile."*

What a privilege it was to speak that night. To perform in front of students, parents, teachers, and community leaders. To come full circle back to my high school where I could hopefully light a fire in a student's belly to strive for a better version of themselves, and not to give up on their dream.

Learning:
As leaders in workplaces, our job is to inspire our colleagues to step up, to speak out, and to share their brilliance in big and small ways.

Pressure into PERFORMANCE

At different phases in life, people put pressure on us. Pressure about who we are and what we can achieve. It takes courage to turn negativity and pressure into performance, but we owe it to ourselves to take those micro-steps, to habitually put things in place, so we can outshine and outperform even our greatest critics.

As Marianne Deborah Williamson said in her book *Personal Power*:

> *"Our deepest fear is not that we are inadequate.*
> *Our deepest fear is that we are powerful beyond measure.*
> ***It is our light, not our darkness, that most frightens us.***
> *We ask ourselves:*
> *"Who am I to be brilliant, gorgeous, talented, fabulous?"*
> *Actually, who are you not to be?*
> ***Your playing small doesn't serve the world.***
> *There is nothing enlightening about shrinking so that other people around you won't feel insecure.*
> *We are born to manifest the glory that is within us.*
> *It is not just in some of us; it is in everyone.*
> ***And as we let our light shine, we unconsciously give other people permission to do the same."***

Reflection

The pressure of being told I was too stupid to reach my dream taught me self-leadership strategies about the impact of stress, how to set boundaries, and how to perform on life's big stage.

What are the pressures you've already experienced in your life?

How have they influenced you?

What have you learnt from them?

How have you transformed those pressures into performance?

I learnt the following *Self-Leadership Strategies* after the PRESSURE from that Careers 'Expert'

1. The Impact Of Stress

The World Health Organisation describes stress as the global health epidemic of the 21st century and have found a fifty-five percent increase in anxiety and depression globally over the last twenty-five years.

We now know that there is a clear link between the stress we experience and our physical and mental ill-health. My pre-HSC itch was a good example of this.

Your body will send you signs and signals about whether or not it is coping with the amount of stress you are trying to deal with. Listen closely. I love this powerful Cherokee proverb that sums this up by saying,

> *"If you listen to your body when it whispers, you won't have to hear it scream."*

Understanding how your brain and body cope and react from professional and personal stress is an impactful lesson to learn. Once you understand the warning signs that it communicates to you, you can intervene on yourself to ensure you don't spiral out of control and become physically and mentally unwell.

When it comes to work, organisations that put their people first will create a distinct competitive advantage when their number one asset - their people - are physically and mentally healthy.

This occurs when stress-reducing policies and education programs that are linked to the strategic objectives of the organisation are adopted as part of normal practice. This will result in better staff retention, less absenteeism, increased productivity, a thriving work culture and a healthier bottom line.

2. Setting Boundaries

It is really hard to say "no". We often say "yes" without properly thinking about the consequences to our time, our health, or our ability to fulfil the request. The pressure we are put under in a workplace to stretch ourselves really thin is a complaint I hear time and time again.

When we consciously say "yes" to things that are not important to us or things that are not right for us, we are unconsciously saying "no" to things that matter most. But fear gets in the way – fear of being demoted, fear of losing a contract, fear of being labelled 'weak', or fear of lost opportunities.

When I decided to say "no" to that school that did not put my personal safety on their priority list, I certainly felt financial fear. This is normal when you take a big step and make changes.

When you find yourself being asked to do something that will compromise your physical or mental health or your ability to accomplish your current responsibilities, here are a few good statements to reply with:

- As much as I would like to help you, I simply can't right now.
- I'm afraid I simply lack the bandwidth right now to commit to doing this.
- I'm really stretched thin right now and I promised myself I wouldn't take on anything else.
- Please come back to me in another month and I will re-visit my schedule to see if I can help.

3. PERFORMANCE

It takes courage to be the headline act in any show. And really, when you think about it, your life is one big Broadway performance.

To perform to the best of your ability, you must take a firm hold of each act and make the decision that you are the one who is creating the script, you are the one who is setting the stage just right, and you are the one who is shining the spotlight where it is needed. When you finally make the decision to curate and influence all the moving parts of your life, then you can give the grand performance you are meant to give.

You might not get a standing ovation first time round, but each time that you lean in, and point that story back to its purpose, you are building your courage, and getting closer to the destination that you deserve.

You may have to become many characters and wear many hats in your life's performance, but each one will build knowledge, skills and bravery to help you stand up, speak out and share your unique brilliance.

Closing Chapter Reminder

Pressure can be transformed into performance once we draw on the positive insights gained from our adversities.

When we courageously embrace the powers of self-leadership and habitually take action in a way that is right for our lives, we can step up and create real and sustainable change.

Over time this means that together, as resilient, optimistic and inspired self-leaders we can make the most impactful difference to our lives, to our workplaces, to our communities, and to our world.

Chapter Five

Disaster into DETERMINATION

"You may not always have a comfortable life and you will not always be able to solve all of the world's problems at once, but don't ever underestimate the importance you can have, because history has shown us that courage can be contagious and hope can take on a life of its own."

Michelle Obama

When I was twenty, I was given the incredible opportunity to spend three months living and working as a teacher in Port Vila, the capital of Vanuatu, an archipelago of islands in the South Pacific. It was absolutely idyllic.

I lived in a small staff house close to the school with a papaya tree at my front and back doors. These trees were abundant with fruit during my time there and my kitchen bench would be lined with these delectable tropical fruits. To this day, whenever I eat papaya I am transported back to this special time in my life. I had no TV or phone which taught me to appreciate the simple things in life such as sitting around a fire and singing songs with my neighbours, or spending hours on a boat watching the horizon as pods of dolphins frolicked in the crystal clear waters next to us. Twice a week, a small van would drive past and beep its horn at 6am to let us know that fresh baguettes and croissants were available. Vanuatu's ties to the French meant that bread and pastries were brought straight from the oven to your door, and nothing would be better than to wake up with these mouth-watering aromas.

I had originally accepted this teaching opportunity in Port Vila because of its location on a warm and sunny tropical island oasis and I pictured myself swanning around in pretty summer dresses, while spending my spare time drinking cocktails out of coconuts. I definitely did that, but as a naïve young woman I hadn't imagined that my time there was going to be such a sliding door moment of my life.

You see, I soon found out that the children of Vanuatu considered going to school as the ultimate privilege and they absolutely loved being there. I am not sure if you have ever been in front of a group, perhaps a conference audience you are presenting to, or a group of investors that you are pitching to, or your colleagues who you are teaching a new strategy to, their interest level in what you are saying can either energise you or deflate you.

In Vanuatu, when you stand in front of a room filled with forty enthusiastic, eager children who have infectious smiles and are willing to do whatever it takes to improve their lives, it fills your heart and soul. I wish I could bottle their enthusiasm and carry it around with me for the rest of my life, so I can open it up during times of trouble and receive that raw, powerful boost that those feelings bring.

I don't have that bottle but I do have the most incredible memories of teaching those very special children. The enjoyment and fulfilment I received from the kids who were like sponges, eager at all times to learn whatever you had to give them, will remain with me till the end of time.

And what made it even more impactful to my life was that I had no idea initially that my smiley, joyful students were sleeping on grass mats, in bamboo huts that looked like a strong gust of wind would blow them over, with no running water or electricity, and with kitchens that comprised of an open fire and a big steel pot. Yet they walked into my class every single morning with the biggest smiles, the whitest shirts, and the determination to make the best of their situations. What did this do for me? I loved them even more. They had nothing to give but gave everything they had. A willingness to be educated and a joyful perspective of life that we could all prosper from.

My absolute favourite part of my time in Port Vila was my after-school dance club. When I first suggested the dance club to the headmaster he thought it would be a great idea for the students but it had never been done before so he was wary on how popular it would be.

I remember standing there in the school hall for the first proposed class all excited about the dance moves I was about to teach, waiting for the students to arrive. But no one did. Oh no. It was going to be a flop before it even started. I began to walk deflated back to my staffroom with my head hanging low but to my absolute delight there were twelve students waiting outside the hall. They had been too shy to be the first ones to step inside. Yah. I had a class.

The goal of that first dance class was to make sure the students got over their awkwardness and shyness of dancing in front of each other, and trusting in me to make the class fun. I am sure you remember your first time at the school disco where everyone waits until somebody else starts dancing. As soon as someone gets grooving, then everyone feels more confident to shake their booties.

And it was no different in that small school hall on that remote island in the middle of the South Pacific. Kids, no matter where you are, act mostly the same. You just need to give them the gentle encouragement and confidence to be themselves. And, wow, once I did that, I was mesmerised by the incredible rhythm and groove that these students had.

The availability of music other than reggae was scarce in Vanuatu, and I soon realised I was going to need more variety, so I asked my sister, Katryna to record onto a cassette tape (yes, that's how old I am – we didn't have any streaming options like we do today) the top forty on a Sunday night from the radio and post it over to me. I would make up dance routines from my small lounge room and then teach the students after school. They LOVED it ... nearly as much as me.

After a few weeks of these dance classes, the word spread of how fabulous they were, and what started as a class with a dozen students for an hour a week, ended up being a class with more than sixty students twice a week for at least two hours. To say they loved it was an understatement. You could feel the anticipation build in the classroom on the days we had dance and by the time the end of school bell rang, you would swear that they were rehearsing for a big Broadway show because the excitement was at such fever pitch. By the end of each dance class I was completely exhausted but it was so worth it because their energy and eagerness was effervescent.

Years later when I bumped into two of my students, they hugged me and then went straight into our favourite dance routine. They had remembered all the moves from over a decade before because they had loved it so much. My heart exploded with pride and my eyes spilled with tears of delight that day to think I could have brought such lasting joy to their lives.

Learning:
Self-leaders know that to have a culture of growth, fun and creativity have to be part of the mix.

Living and working in Vanuatu was definitely a sliding-door moment for me and I knew deep down that at some stage in my life I would be back there to continue my love of providing life-changing opportunities to these amazing children in the best way I could – through education.

Little did I know that it would take the massacre of eight hundred thousand Rwandan Tutsis to lead me back to this place that had stolen a piece of my heart.

When I made the decision that you read about in that previous chapter to leave teaching in Sydney, I worked really hard to save enough money to travel overseas. For nine months I worked as a teacher five days a week, and worked as a waitress in a fancy-pants Sydney restaurant six nights a week. I bravely left Australia with a one-way ticket to Greece and no definite plan, but a strong belief that I would fall on my feet and everything would work out okay.

It would be fair to say that when I left I was pretty insular, not very worldly, and I certainly did not follow politics and global current affairs as closely as I should have. After two years of backpacking around Europe, UK, Ireland, and the Middle East, as well as living and working in London (like pretty much most Aussies do at some stage) we were off to South East Africa. When I say "we", I mean the boyfriend I had at the time.

Seeing the mountain gorillas of Zaire (now Democratic Republic of Congo) in all their glory had been a dream of mine for years. I remember even as a child, being absolutely fascinated at the zoo with all the monkeys and chimpanzees. They are so human-like. Mum told me that when I was a little girl in my pram we were watching the big old mountain gorilla at Sydney's Taronga Zoo, and he was obviously in a bad mood (probably because he was in a cage and not in the jungle - don't start me on that), and he threw a big handful of poo through the bars onto my pram. Apparently, despite being covered in poo, I found it all very funny.

Learning:
Don't let being shat on spoil your day!

During the planning of this backpacking trip I knew that I would go across to Zaire to see these magical human-like furry kings of the jungle - somehow, some way.

We wanted our money to last as long as we could so we could see Africa in all its raw beauty and therefore we were prepared to eat, sleep, and travel in ways that I would never consider doing now. Of course when you are young, naïve, footloose and fancy-free, you think everything will be okay at all times and that life is there for you to enjoy.

Learning:
It's important to understand where and how you fit into the world.
Self-leadership is not just about self.
It is about how you impact others around you.

Getting to see the mountain gorillas of Zaire was not something that we felt we could do on our own, so we booked an overland truck company to take us to our destination. Beginning in Nairobi we drove through the northern parts of Kenya, across the plateaus of Uganda, and then finally into the jungles of Zaire.

This was June 1994, and for one hundred days since the 7th April, Hutus had slaughtered eight hundred thousand Rwandan Tutsis. Even for a country with such turbulent history as Rwanda, the scale and speed of the slaughter left its people reeling.

The despicable part of this story is that I don't remember thinking about this. I also don't remember the overland company talking to us about the fact that we were going to be travelling right through the refugee camps where hundreds of thousands of displaced people (who had probably watched their family members, neighbours, and friends being raped, tortured, and killed), would be.

How on earth were we allowed to travel into this area? Us privileged westerners who got to have such an amazing life that we could spend our days travelling through such horror while those around us suffered such horrendous loss and trauma.

Grrrrr.

This disaster has marked me forever on so many levels.

Firstly, because of my own naivety, ignorance, and the fact I was unaware of this disastrous event. How could I have been so caught up in my own travel plans, so selfish with my life, that I had not paid attention to this human cruelty? What does it say about me as a person?

Secondly, that a travel company was prepared to take our money despite the instability of the area and the fact that our presence would be such a "slap in the face" to those who were suffering so deeply.

But it is this third reason that has impacted me the most and made me determined to do things so differently.

While we were spending time in Uganda, waiting for permission to continue, we spent days walking alongside and being amongst the displaced Rwandans. I will never forget the shock of seeing with my own eyes the ripple effect of such a brutal genocide. I would never know until much later the extent of what they had all suffered, but when you are looking into eyes that are devoid of life, you know that the level of cruelty that they have witnessed will never leave them.

Of course, every humanitarian not-for-profit organisation was there. And this is when my third determination lesson started. The lesson was so strong that it stayed in my head and in my heart for seven years before I could unpack it, learn from it and have the courage to do it differently.

One day we were walking past a hotel. It was probably one that we would rate as a two star here in Australia, but in Uganda it was considered pretty posh. At the time it stood out like an oasis in the desert, a lone beacon for a lost ship because to the Rwandan refugees looking in, it represented everything they could not have. This hotel was a compound, with a high guarded fence all around it, where only the privileged could take shelter.

There was a big circular driveway in front of that hotel, like what I remember from the movie *Gone With The Wind,* and parked nose to toe on that driveway were about twenty brand-spanking-new white four-wheel drives from all the well-known aid organisations. This seemed so wrong to me. Surely money was better spent on helping refugees rather than on purchasing brand-new, top-of-the-range SUVs? I mean, the camps we had seen had row after row of makeshift tents squashed side-by-side and they urgently needed more water, sanitation and medication for the growing amount of people who were desperately looking for a safe haven.

Looking through that fence, you could see the aid workers sitting comfortably on the shaded verandah, laughing and joking while sipping their drinks. This picture of the haves and the have-nots made me feel so angry, but it wasn't until later that evening that this anger rose to a boiling point.

You see, we were out and about looking for somewhere to eat. We wanted a break from being with the others on our overland trip so we could discuss how this whole screwed up situation was making us feel. It was truly an unexpected and horrific situation that was causing a whole plethora of emotions that we didn't really know how to deal with.

As we were wandering the streets, we met a couple of New Zealand pilots who were working for one of the big aid organisations. They realised we were Aussies and therefore wanted to share some antipodean banter and help us to find somewhere to eat. The little 'restaurant' we discovered was a makeshift thatched palm-leaf hut with no tables or chairs but with long logs to sit on. Perfect. We shared a simple bowl of rice and vegetables and chatted about what was going on around us. It was during this conversation that I realised that I might actually punch someone tonight – for the first time in my life.

You see, these pilots were proudly explaining that they had been staying in that posh hotel for twenty-eight days and had done nothing for the plight of the people. They thought it was funny that they had spent their days going from buffet lunch to buffet dinner with a dozen cold beers to link those events. It made me feel sick to my stomach. I mean, where was the donated money going? Food, cars, and beer? Surely there should have been someone who was checking where the money went. Such waste.

I was disgusted by this attitude and couldn't believe what I had just heard. Here we were feeling so guilty about our privileged lives while surrounded by such desperation but in front of us were two people thinking it was great that they were having such a party in the middle of a humanitarian disaster.

Learning:
The world watches you and the decisions you make even when you think no-one important is looking.

I kept thinking, why wouldn't they be doing everything they could to help these poor displaced people? Why would they not give them the help and support they so desperately needed? I felt my anger start to build inside of me with each "why" that I asked. I clearly remember my rage as I stood up shaking with anger with my hands clenched as tight as possible. I am not sure if it was my sudden scream of "why" or the fact that I knocked over my boyfriend's bowl of rice that made the two pilots jump back in shock and start to call me all sorts of names… *"psycho bitch, dumb aussie, nutcase"*. I stood shaking with fury but their words washed over me like water off a duck's back. I mean, what the male students used to call me at that first school I had been sent to was much worse than that and made these Kiwi pilots look like two nuns on a spring morning singing hymns. Their words meant nothing; it was their inability to notice the human suffering that was surrounding us at every turn that affected me most.

They quickly departed once they realised we did not find their behaviour anything other than despicable and irresponsible. They had the means to help suffering human beings, but they didn't. Arrggggh. It still makes me so angry. How can life be so unfair? The only reason that these Rwandan refugees had to endure this 'hell on earth' situation was because they had been born into their particular culture. It was not their fault. And then here are hundreds of the privileged born in a western country who are supposed to be helping them, but they are not. Again that question, why?

When we arrived back to our overland group and told them what had happened, the tour leader sat me down and explained about how there was just so much red tape in situations like this. Bureaucracy and regulation overtook common sense and a simple signature that was required from someone in an office back in a first world country, had probably delayed the whole operation.

This is where I learnt the true meaning of 'so near yet so far.'

The ongoing inhumane conditions these people were suffering through could have ended by a simple stroke of a pen, but instead all the supplies were kept under lock and key in that guarded posh hotel.

So how did this momentous wrongdoing affect me later in my life? How did I turn this story of disaster into a story of determination?

Well the only positive I could feasibly take from such a tragedy was the iron clad promise that I made to myself that if I ever got to be in a position where I could help those who were less fortunate than me, I would do whatever was required to take action and make a difference. I would never let small hurdles stop me as I had seen first-hand the prolonged suffering that is caused from inaction and ineffective processes. I wasn't to know at the time that I would definitely be called upon to uphold this promise to myself, and that it would shape my future in years to come.

In 2001, eleven years after my initial time as a teacher in Port Vila, and seven years after the Rwandan genocide, this opportunity arose and I was able to fulfil this promise in a rather indirect way, through the personal training business that I had begun in Sydney.

I saw a small advertisement about the Vanuatu Island Relay, an annual event that celebrates Vanuatu's independence from France and Britain in 1980. A team of ten participants would run or walk one section each of the one hundred and forty-eight-kilometre circumference of Efate, which is where their capital, Port Vila is located, to symbolically link all the villages around the island. The first participant completes approximately fourteen kilometres in the first section and hands over the baton to their teammate. The second participant does the same, and so on, until all ten participants have made their way relay-style around the island.

Being a participant in this spectacular event would mean you walked or trotted or jogged through tropical jungles and bougainvillea-lined streets with giggling children ready to give you high-fives as you go past. Each village would make their section of the road beautiful with palm fronds and flowers and greet you with local string bands that sang you songs of encouragement. I have participated in dozens of incredible fun runs/walks in my life but this one has to be the most unique, uplifting and scenic event of its kind in the world.

In 2001, the twenty first anniversary of Vanuatu's Independence, they had decided to open up this national event to overseas groups. I thought this would be a great opportunity to combine my two loves - movement and education - so I organised a *Jump Start* team.

Learning:
Sometimes it takes much longer than you think before the opportunities to shine really show up.
Self-leaders are patient.

We were the first overseas team to "compete" in this amazing event, and it was, in fact, the start of my determination lesson. Once I began to bring teams over I was again touched deeply by the infectious smiles and the beautiful family values of the ni-vanuatu (the people of Vanuatu) and knew that I needed to take advantage of this opportunity to provide education resources and programs for the children. All the incredible memories from eleven years before had come flooding back and the ray of sunshine in my heart was beaming brightly.

Disaster into DETERMINATION

Little did I know that seeing that small advertisement in the paper about this fun run would bring me back to the place that filled me with such joy and start the wheels of motion for my beloved *Jump Start Foundation*. As a not-for-profit organisation we began partnering with local communities in Vanuatu to provide life-changing opportunities through education. Our belief was that everyone deserves the right to be educated and that education empowers people to improve socio-economic conditions for their families, communities, countries and future generations.

Never let anyone tell you that starting a foundation is easy. In fact, where were my mentors when I needed them? Ha ha. Starting a foundation from scratch is pretty much like being at the base of a massive snow-capped mountain with only leather sandals to trek with. The start is not too bad but every time you get a little closer to the top, you hit some ice and then slide all the way back down. You are completely frustrated, have painful blisters on your feet and chaffing on your inner thighs that drives you nuts. Raising money for overseas projects without any government funding nor any paid workers is tough. I honestly cannot count how many times I thought we would need to give it all away because whenever we had reached the top of one mountain, we could see that we had many more slippery mountains to conquer.

Jump Start Foundation started out from humble beginnings by raising money throughout the year before we went over to Port Vila for the annual Independence Day relay event. We had garage sales, raffles, and silent auctions, and received sporadic donations by generous supporters.

After much consultation with community leaders and the education department, we began by providing student literacy packs and teaching resources to two remote primary schools that needed it most. In the first few years we annually provided about ten removalist size boxes filled with stationery, reading books, pens and pencils. Air Vanuatu recognised all the great work we were doing and soon became a sponsor allowing us to have a lot of extra free cargo on this annual trip which meant we could instead take forty to fifty boxes with us each time.

Our education work expanded into delivering empowerment workshops, plus sport, travel, and education sponsorships to teenage girls. The ultimate achievement was when we built a community library on the remote island of Tanna, a place where literacy was way behind the national average.

This incredible library project took over one thousand volunteer hours and involved hundreds of generous people from both sides of the Pacific with the goal of fostering community participation and developing community ownership.

By involving local people in every step from conception to delivery it meant that everyone could feel pride, respect and part ownership of the project. And although my builder hubby kept telling me that he could take his team and tools over and get the library finished in a few weeks, we made the decision that we would use local materials, local tradesmen and local decision-makers throughout the entire process.

Timber came from the forests behind the school and was milled not far away; three thousand concrete blocks were hand-made by one of the local elders; the boys from the Trade School who were studying to be carpenters helped to build the library (under supervision) as part of their practical component of their certification; a local electrician and his son wired it all up; the school held fundraisers such as talent nights and sold island greens to raise a proportion of the total cost; mamas and papas collected coral from the beach for the concrete slab; fifty giggling students stood in a line on a hot day passing a bucket of water from the one tap in the school to the concrete mixer; the teachers filled sandbags of dirt to use as a filler; they held Parent and Citizen meetings while I was in Vanuatu so we could discuss any potential problems and make decisions together about the next steps; mamas made beautiful curtains and floral arrangements on completion ready for our big opening celebration; and a young, local woman was trained as the in-house librarian.

The library was a real milestone for this part of Vanuatu bringing the first new children's books ever to the community and dramatically increasing the range of choices available to students. It brought much needed learning resources for the children of Tanna, as well as their families, the wider community and future generations.

Over the fourteen years that I was president, I took fifteen running and walking teams to participate in the Vanuatu Island Relay; over three hundred enthusiastic volunteers to work on our education projects; two life-changing student holiday programs from Methodist Ladies College, Melbourne; and more than ten thousand kilograms worth of literacy resources for students and teachers.

I must add here that Jump Start Foundation could only do all its incredible work because we had the combined help of many, many generous and caring people. If it were not for each and every one of the management committee and all the other volunteers who worked tirelessly to reach our goal, there is no way we would have achieved so much. I still feel an enormous amount of gratitude to dozens, in fact hundreds, of individuals, whose kind and big-hearted actions meant we could make the difference that we set out to make.

How does this story of determination in Vanuatu link back to that story of disaster in Rwanda? Well, I had promised myself back then that if I were ever in a position where I could help those who were less fortunate than me, I would do whatever was required to take action and make a difference. This was top of mind during my entire time of being the president of *Jump Start Foundation*.

I did not want outsiders to look at our foundation and wonder if we were living a great life off donations that were supposed to be going to the children.

I did not want outsiders to look at our foundation and wonder if the projects we were involved in were actually getting the appropriate funds.

I did not want outsiders to look at our foundation and wonder if the people who needed the help most were actually receiving the help our donors were generously giving.

I felt so strongly about this, and it became one of our leading values, that apart from compliance fees that we had to give to the Australian Government, one hundred percent of our donations would go to the projects so that the people who needed them most would benefit and thrive because of this promise.

Learning:
Self-leaders are honest and value-driven.
They keep to their word and are transparent with their actions.

None of us took any money for the thousands of hours we gave, and we had dozens and dozens of supporters who generously gifted us, at no cost, their experience, talents, services, and products just so we could uphold this important value.

In fact, when Cyclone Pam devastated the country in 2015, we received a large amount of donations from people around the world because of this particular fact. In the Facebook groups of concerned global citizens that we became a part of, it was really interesting to see how astounded people were that we gave all their donated money to our projects.

In my mind, this is what "not-for-profit" should really mean. Of course, I know this is idealistic and when it is a big beast of a global aid organisation, you need good people to make it run well, and these good people should be paid.

In the case of *Jump Start Foundation*, I was determined to ensure that we were completely transparent about our donations and where they were being directed.

In workplaces when employees feel disconnected from the values of their employer, when they don't believe in the purpose of the organisation, a breakdown of trust occurs, and disengagement sets in. Unfortunately, disengagement fuels sarcasm, bickering, backstabbing, and a lack of productivity.

Great self-leaders always make sure they have the right people in their teams. Ones who believe in what they believe in. Ones that value what they value.

Self-leaders walk their talk and practise what they preach.

Self-leaders are the role models that others look up to.

Learning:
Every day, self-leaders demonstrate the behaviours that they expect from others.

Every person at every level of an organisation should be accountable to the values that have been set in place. Those that don't believe in them should not be there. Those that don't embrace them should not be there.

Self-leaders are not able to work in a place where they feel disconnected to the core values because they need to be authentic and honest to who they are at all times. And this is why organisations who encourage self-leadership will always be more successful than other organisations. The reason for this is that if you give people the opportunity to step up, speak out, and share their brilliance, then you will reap the rewards.

Allowing your people to be self-leaders does take courage: you have to trust in their abilities and motivations and self-assigned direction because this is when self-leaders are at their best.

Reflection

The Rwandan Genocide disaster taught me self-leadership strategies on how to be accountable, how to be trustworthy and transparent in all my dealings, and how to be determined to shape my life into one I would be proud of.

What are the disasters you've already experienced in your life?

How have they influenced you?

What have you learnt from them?

How have you transformed those disasters into determination?

I learnt these *Self-Leadership Strategies* from the Rwandan Genocide DISASTER

1. Accountability

We all have to be accountable to someone. But first we have to be accountable to ourselves.

Self-leaders portray behaviours that others admire and they comprehend that not only are they role models to their team members but they are also accountable to them. It is a two-way relationship. Team members are accountable to their leaders, and leaders are accountable to their team members.

Who was keeping those pilots accountable in Rwanda? Who was checking to see if they were wasting money that had been generously donated? How would the leaders of that organisation have felt knowing that their team members were displaying such poor behaviour? Why was there no accountability?

2. Trust and Transparency

When I created my foundation, I never wanted to be in a situation where I wasn't completely trusted by my stakeholders.

Trust is something you earn, and you can only gain it when you are completely transparent.

To be a trusted leader, transparency is required in all your dealings. Being open and honest with your decisions, being vulnerable, and walking your talk, is what will propel you to heights you never imagined.

3. DETERMINATION

I am a fairly passionate person who has strong views on right and wrong. When I see injustice, I feel determined to do something about it.

It took seven years before I could apply the self-leadership learnings from the disaster of the Rwandan genocide to my own not-for-profit, but every minute of those next fourteen years that I was the president I was determined that anyone who worked with us would know that we could be trusted, we were transparent, and we were accountable to all our stakeholders.

This determination has also been applied to my businesses over the last two decades. The reality is that people will only do business with those they know, like, and trust so if you have strong values that your staff, customers and stakeholders respect, then great opportunities, the right people, and better results will always come your way.

To gain the edge in a business sense, you need to have the courage to be accountable to those at every level, and be transparent in everything you do. This is when, as a self-leader, you can really step up and gain the admiration that you deserve.

Closing Chapter Reminder

Disasters can be transformed into determination once we draw on the positive insights gained from our adversities.

When we courageously embrace the powers of self-leadership and habitually take action in a way that is right for our lives, we can step up and create real and sustainable change.

Over time this means that together, as resilient, optimistic and inspired self-leaders we can make the most impactful difference to our lives, to our workplaces, to our communities, and to our world.

Chapter Six

Stupidity into STABILITY

"When stability becomes a habit, maturity and clarity follow."

B.K.S. Iyengar

When you are young and fancy-free, you sometimes believe you are invincible. Ha. You take risks that you shouldn't, and you push the line when it comes to safety. Of course, once you are older and wiser, you can see how this belief is actually stupidity.

During my five months of backpacking in South Eastern Africa, we started to take risks that we shouldn't have. Getting around Africa can be pretty difficult if you are not part of an overland package tour. We had done this earlier in this trip, but decided it wasn't really for us, and wanted to be a bit more free about when we travelled and who we travelled with.

When you arrive somewhere that is spectacular, there is nothing better than being able to decide you want to stay there for an extra night or an extra three nights or an extra seven nights. To have that freedom is a once-in-a-lifetime experience, and we knew that this was the way we wanted to see Africa.

Of course, to have this type of freedom meant that we had to put our trust in the fact that all would be okay. We started to take local buses from destination to destination, which really meant we could get to know the locals so much more because this was how they travelled - on the back of utes and jam-packed into minibuses.

When you are standing shoulder to shoulder for three hours with someone, or hanging on for dear life together on the back of an overcrowded ute, conversations are colourful and honest and interesting. You learn so much more about your fellow commuter's lives, their families, and their work circumstances.

Learning:
Self-leaders converse with a variety of people of all ages, races, gender, and belief systems because they know that golden nuggets of information can happen when you least expect it.

One of the conversations that stands out so much in my mind was telling a man in Malawi about "the dole" that we get here in Australia. He could not believe that a government would actually give you money when you haven't got a job. This concept was so incredulous to him, and it made me realise how much we take for granted.

He had been trying desperately to get work for two years. He had a new baby and felt desperate to be able to keep his wife and baby housed, fed, and safe. His parents were helping them but he wanted to stand on his own two feet. The fact that Australians who were in this same situation were handed money every fortnight was truly out of this world to him.

There was another situation that I will never forget when we were travelling on the back of a truck in Tanzania. A young mother was travelling with her four-year-old who looked very close to dying. The little girl was as stiff as a board, her eyes were enormous and staring into space, you could see she had a high fever, and looked to be in a terrible amount of pain. Her Mum was trying to breastfeed her but she was too sick and lethargic to take any milk.

We learnt that the little girl most likely had cerebral malaria and the Mum was trying desperately to get her daughter some medical help. Everyone else on the back of that truck seemed to take this in their stride, because unfortunately this was a far more normal occurrence for them. For us though, to see the desperation in this Mum's eyes as she nursed her little girl, knowing that the likelihood of her surviving was not great, was heartbreaking.

And a reality check.

How lucky we are in our country to have the healthcare that we have. Where the majority of us can access doctors within a few kilometres of where we live, and emergency doctors that constantly make difficult decisions that save our lives. The fact that the infant mortality rate in Tanzania is ten times what we have in Australia is shocking.

Learning:
Self-leaders can't stand it when things are unfair or unjust, and they often try to remedy the situation.

The last trip we did by local transport before we decided to take our risk-taking and stupidity to another level was a long bus trip from Dar es Salaam in Tanzania, through Mozambique, into Malawi. It was an epic twenty-eight hour journey on a rusty old 'coach' with more drama than I could have ever imagined.

We only stopped four times during the entire journey and that was only because we begged for a toilet stop. Girls on one side of the bus and boys on the other. The second time I was squatting amongst all the African mamas, they all started to laugh at me. I wasn't sure why until I stood up and realised I hadn't hoisted my skirt up far enough, and had been weeing all over it. Sitting in your cold, wet, stinky wee for hours and hours is pretty disgusting.

The bus was so weighed down with all the luggage that it could only go about forty kilometres per hour, which led to robbers jumping on top and cutting the ropes and stealing the boxes and bags and suitcases. Thankfully we had our backpacks with us under our feet, but this did mean for twenty-eight hours we were sitting with very bent knees, which caused pins and needles and cramps.

Another incident on that unforgettable trip was when a husband and wife felt they needed the collective advice of everyone on the bus to help them with their marriage problems. The bus pulled over and for the next forty-five minutes we all got to give our two-pennies worth to the young couple who ended up being very pleased with the outcome. Hilarious.

After that marathon trip we started hitchhiking.

Yes, I know, how STUPID. But at the time, it was such an adventure and we were meeting the most interesting people who were really generous and kind and wonderful. Well, that was how it was in Malawi, Zimbabwe, and Botswana. But that is when we should have stopped.

We didn't though because it then became a bit of a challenge to see if we could hitch ourselves all the way down to Cape Town in South Africa, which was our final destination. We had already covered about one thousand five hundred kilometres hitching rides; surely we could complete this last part.

I was lucky enough to have some family friends, Trisha and Bill, who lived in Durban. They had been our neighbours as I was growing up but had moved to South Africa years before.

This was 1994, and in the May of that year, Nelson Mandela was elected as the president of South Africa. In the lead-up to this election, we had been in a lot of contact with Trisha and Bill to get their opinion on whether they thought the country would be safe following these historical elections. At the time, no one knew what was going to happen. Would Nelson Mandela be elected? If he wasn't, would there be civil war? If he was, would there be serious repercussions for the white population? It was all so unknown.

Luckily for everyone, this election was a peaceful and inspiring one that brought the country together, humanity together, and we all felt that this new chapter of South Africa's history would be positive. And therefore, it was okay for us to travel there.

We stayed with Bill and Trisha for a week. How nice it was to sleep in a real bed, wash clothes in a machine, and eat homemade food at a dinner table. I'll never, ever forget Durban's delicious Bunny Chows. Durban has one of the largest populations of Indians outside of India, which means, amongst many things, that their curries are delectable. A Bunny Chow, though, is something quite unique. You take an un-sliced loaf of freshly baked bread, pull out the entire filling from the middle, pour your favourite curry into the hollow, and then dip the pulled out bread into the curry. YUM.

Learning:
Self-leaders love to try new things.
New food, new destinations, new marketing models, new recruitment processes, and new business opportunities.

Anyway, after we finally got our travel legs back on, we wanted to head off south and make our way along the coast until we got to Cape Town. We thought that this was an awesome plan, and a perfect way to end the last three to four weeks of our adventure. South Africa's coastline looked beautiful. It was rugged, natural, and dappled with places to scuba dive, drink wine, and see wildlife. Could it get any better than that?

Apparently though, for us to get to all of those amazing areas, we would have to firstly travel inland and then south otherwise we would need to go through the Transkei area, which was completely off limits in regards to safety.

Bill and Trisha spoke to us for days about this. That if we were dead set on hitching (which we still stupidly were), then we must, must, must go across to Bloemfontein (inland) and then head south to East London, where we could then safely travel along the coast to Cape Town. This was the only way ... in their minds, because the alternative, through the Transkei, was far too risky.

We talked this through dozens of times, but we thought they were being paranoid white South Africans. We had been travelling for months alongside Africans and they had shown us nothing but kindness, generosity, and friendship. Why would this Transkei area be any different? We were certain they were overreacting. And plus, to go the way they suggested was over twelve hundred kilometres, and to go direct the way we wanted was about six hundred and sixty kilometres. A mammoth difference. In time. In kilometres. In effort. In accommodation we would have to pay for.

This is the point where our stupidity and stubbornness nearly got us killed. You see, even though our friends had constantly advised us against travelling through the Transkei region, we told them that was the way we were going and nothing they could say would change our minds.

Learning:
Listening to experienced, trusted advisors who have your best interests at heart is smart.

I can still remember that day when they dropped us off early in the morning at a spot on the far side of the city that led straight to the freeway that would take us to our destination. Up to the last goodbyes they were still trying to convince us to take a safer route but our stubbornness was having none of that – we had effortlessly hitchhiked for fifteen hundred kilometres up to now and we were sure this would be no different. How wrong we were.

Their last desperate recommendation to us was to make sure we got a hitch that went right through the Transkei and out the other end. DO NOT get off part of the way and try and get another hitch. Doing this will put your life at risk. DO NOT do it. We felt that this was a good compromise and since we had always had such good luck with our hitchhiking in the past, this was a warning we could easily heed, as we were sure that someone would be going right through to the other side.

We were dropped off at 7am with high hopes, a few snacks, a bottle of water, and an eagerness to get started on this new chapter of our travel adventures.

8am came and went.

10am came and went.

11.30am came and went.

No one was going through to the other side. Everyone was just going to Umtata (now known as Mthatha), the place we were warned definitely not to get off at.

What should we do? It had been a long day just standing there. We knew we needed to get this hitch before 1pm, otherwise we would arrive at our destination after dark. This is when we made a stupid decision to get the next hitch no matter where it was going and then see what would happen from there.

STUPID. STUPID. STUPID.

The next car that pulled up was a man who could drop us off in Umtata so we decided to take that chance because otherwise we would have to turn back and admit defeat.

Learning:
The best self-leaders are not afraid to admit their mistakes.

Our ride was with a fabulous Scottish guy who had been working in the Reserve Police Service, which is a volunteer group that supports the South African Police. I could see by his reaction that he was surprised that we were travelling through the Transkei. He actually thought we must know someone in Umtata to be going there.

We heard lots of colourful stories from our Scottish saviour about his life back in Scotland, about how he ended up as a volunteer in South Africa, and we definitely thought we had struck lucky with this hitch. That was until he started to scare us a bit about the dangers of Umtata and the stories of violence and rape that had been going on in this area, especially to female foreigners who dared come through. He said we should have listened to our friends back in Durban because there was no real 'law' where we were headed.

My boyfriend and I looked at each other and forced half-smiles onto our faces, trying to convince each other that it was all going to be okay. I've never been able to disguise my true feelings very well. In fact, my face is like an open book. Every emotion is there to be read. I'd be such a hopeless poker player. My face must have portrayed the mounting fear that I was experiencing, because my boyfriend reached across to squeeze my hand and we privately clung to each other for the remainder of the trip.

As we got closer to our destination, he asked us if we had a knife. I thought he meant it as a bit of a joke and I said, of course we do, I have my Swiss Army Knife. He laughed at this and said he didn't mean that, he meant did we have a proper knife? Since we didn't he said to open the glove box and take one of his. The one he gave us was about twenty centimetres long with a carved wooden handle and a mighty big blade. In fact, I actually kept this knife for the following twenty-five years because it signified such a momentous (and stupid) day of my life.

At this point, I really did start to worry. I mean, what on earth would we need a knife for? To protect ourselves, he told us. What was about to happen in this place? What had we got ourselves into? So bloody stupid. We asked our Scottish driver if there was anywhere else he could drop us as we now realised the trouble we were in. He said there was nowhere because he was going to work at a remote village about twenty kilometres out of town and we would never get a lift from there due to its remoteness. It was too late to turn around. We were stuck.

As we drove up the main street of Umtata I firstly thought that this is not that bad. It didn't look a lot different to the other African places I had been in. People were going about their business or just hanging around the shops.

With some trepidation, we said goodbye to our Scottish friend when he dropped us off in the middle of town. As I watched the tail lights of his car disappear up the road, I immediately knew we were in danger. Have you ever had the hairs on the back of your head stand up instantly? Every little nerve ending in my body felt on high alert and it seemed like the entire town was staring at us and closing in on us.

We stood out like a sore thumb - stupid, white backpackers alone in the middle of a dangerous and violent city. We quickly put on our backpacks and started walking up the centre of the road, trying not to show how petrified we were.

It firstly started with whistles and woohoos from a few men walking in step beside us, but this quickly grew to twenty to thirty men and boys shouting and laughing and pointing and egging each other on, in that mob kind of way.

I thought, this is it. I gripped that knife we had been given which I had hidden on the inside of my jacket. Would I be forced to use it? Would I know what to do with it? Would I actually be brave enough to pull it out?

That intense emotion of panic and dread that I felt that afternoon has again washed over me as I am writing these words. It was just so so scary and not only did I feel a great sense of hopelessness but I also felt so bloody stupid for not listening to all the warnings that we had been given. Most of all though, there was an overpowering sensation of complete and utter fear.

As the mob started to close in on us, I felt like the zebras we had seen only months before in the Masai Mara game park. Those striking, peaceful animals would be going about their own business, grazing in the long grass, when a pride of lions would surround them and close in ready to pounce.

Then out of nowhere, this army-looking vehicle sped past and the men shouted out of the windows. I wasn't sure exactly who they were shouting at or who they were until they came past again, screeching to a halt and blocking the middle of the road in front of us. I thought for sure this is it. I am about to die.

Two men jumped out of the four-wheel drive wearing full army gear and one was carrying a machine gun. They pointed the gun at the mob behind us and screamed at us to get in the car. I thought we were about to be abducted and we both hesitated.

The driver of the four-wheel drive leaped out with his machine gun and screamed that if we did not get in the car we would die. OMFG. It was absolutely terrifying. We had no choice and as we shuffled onto the back seat I was convinced we were about to become the next story of foreigners being murdered in this area.

The two men jumped back in the car and as we sped away, they were screaming at us about what the hell we were doing at this time of the day in Umtata as the only foreigners in one of the country's most dangerous areas. They were what was known as the "Armed Forces Reaction Group." I suppose like a Special Forces unit, and they weren't abducting us but they were actually saving us. They said that if we had stayed there by ourselves for another twenty minutes we would be dead.

GULP.

What we had been told over and over again by our friends in Durban had been true. It wasn't a fabricated story or an exaggerated story. It was the truth. This was a seriously dangerous place that we had no right to be in and we were just so stupid to think that we knew better than people who had lived here for years.

> ***Learning:***
> ***Don't ignore warning signs that various people give you just because it's not what you want to hear.***

Our new "escort" drove us out of town and waited with us to make sure we were safe. They said to give it twenty minutes but if we didn't get the right hitch by then we could stay with them for the night. There was only twenty minutes left before it would be dark and after that it was far too risky. With about one minute of light left, we got the perfect hitch from someone who was going straight to where we needed to go.

PHEW.

We were lucky that our stupidity had not ended up costing our lives that day. It was a massive reality check about our own mortality and our place in this world.

Reflection

The good news is that stupidly hitchhiking into dangerous places eventually taught me self-leadership strategies on how to surround myself with trusted mentors, how to understand the difference between irrational risk-taking and informed risk-taking, and how stability is a trait that should be admired.

What are the stupid, irrational things you have already done in your life?

How have they influenced you?

What have you learnt from them?

How have you transformed that stupidity into stability?

I learnt the following
Self-Leadership Strategies
from my
Hitch-Hiking STUPIDITY

1. Mentors

There are many people in your life who want to see you succeed.

Who are they? Write them down now. Don't only think about the people who will give you nothing but praise, but also consider the ones who you can rely on to give thoughtful, insightful recommendations. They are like your brains trust. They desperately want to see you succeed and are willing to look at your challenges with fresh eyes. They will stretch you and question you until the right answer appears for you.

Your mentors or brains trust can come from all parts of your life - your work environment (past and present), your family, your friends, or your sporting/musical/hobby group. Including the people who know you from a variety of places will ensure you get a variety of opinions because they all know the varying shades of your personality, your strengths and your limitations.

Mentors are there for you during the good times and the bad, and are willing to gently advise you when your inner compass is off track.

Self-leaders know that having diverse conversations with trusted advisors will keep them on the right path at work and in life.

Since that near-death experience in South Africa, I have definitely learnt the value of surrounding myself with trusted mentors who I can reach out to when I need unbiased opinions during my times of trouble.

2. Irrational Risk-Taking vs Informed Risk-Taking

To stretch ourselves so we can achieve bigger dreams often takes a little risk. What we know though is that there is a big difference between irrational risk-taking and informed risk-taking.

When you are a young backpacker and you choose crazy, stupid, irrational risk-taking behaviours (such as hitchhiking into areas that everyone warned you against), then you hold your breath and hope that you make it out the other end.

If you are that irrational with your decisions at work, not only can you negatively impact yourself but you can also negatively impact your colleagues.

As a self-leader in a workplace, you will need to (and want to) take risks at times. Informed risk-taking means you have thought through the consequences of your actions and have decided that the outcomes are worthwhile.

Unfortunately though, in many organisations, you find leaders who are willing to leave a trail of destruction as they push their way to the top. They ignore all the warning signs that signify that what they are doing is not in the best interest of anyone other than themselves.

The best self-leaders will take risks because they love the challenge of new experiences and understand that to keep moving forward they need to lean in and push the boundaries a little bit. But they will never choose risks that put their colleagues or their organisations in harm's way. They listen carefully and watch closely for warning signs that indicate they are on a risky and unstable path, and they re-calibrate their goals to ensure the psychological safety of their team and the financial safety of their organisation.

This is why organisations need self-leaders who have the courage to instinctively take informed risks and create new opportunities that others wouldn't consider. When this occurs it leads to innovation, awards, growth, employer of choice status, and improved profits.

3. STABILITY

Stability is not a trait that everyone strives towards. Many professionals do not want to be known as being stable, because this often has negative connotations and presumes they are old-fashioned, out-dated and obsolete.

The fact of the matter is that teams and organisations need people who others can rely on. To be seen as that rock, that trustworthy person who is attentive and consistently gives thoughtful guidance, is a skill that should be admired.

In this volatile, ever-changing world that we live in, to be someone whom others can depend upon and trust is a sign of a talented self-leader. When you combine informed risk-taking with confident, stable guidance, not only will your colleagues look up to you and respect the decisions you make, but the opportunities you create for yourself will keep you on the path that leads to great destinations.

Closing Chapter Reminder

Stupidity can eventually teach us the benefits of stability once we draw on the positive insights gained from our adversities.

When we courageously embrace the powers of self-leadership and habitually take action in a way that is right for our lives, we can step up and create real and sustainable change.

Over time this means that together, as resilient, optimistic and inspired self-leaders we can make the most impactful difference to our lives, to our workplaces, to our communities, and to our world.

Chapter Seven

Setbacks into SELF-CARE

"It takes courage to say yes to rest and play in a culture where exhaustion is seen as a status symbol."

Brene Brown

It was a belated long-service-leave holiday that I had promised myself after ten years of business. Life got in the way a bit so it was closer to the thirteen-year mark before we left.

Firstly, we travelled to Dublin to visit my husband Ken's family, then a driving holiday through Spain and Portugal, back to Dublin for a few more visits with all the cousins, aunties, and uncles (there are a lot – it is Ireland), and then to Thailand on our way home.

Five weeks is a long time to be away from a small business and I was pretty worried at first about how my business would "survive" without me being there. I knew that I had an excellent team who supported me finally having this big break, but I needed to be clear on how it would all work. The great lesson on being away for that long is that it forces you to get really smart about your systems and processes and scheduling before you go. I worked extra hard for about six weeks prior to leaving to ensure that everyone in my team knew exactly what their responsibility was while I was away, and what they had to do on a daily basis.

Learning:
Self-leaders understand that they are not the only one in the world who can do things well.
They can delegate and trust in the people around them because they have made it clear what the expectations are.

Although I didn't know it at the time, delegating all the components of my business for that five-week holiday meant that everything was in place for the next eighteen months when I couldn't really work due to the setback I was about to experience.

After an incredible European holiday we were to stop off on our way home in Thailand and return to the *Elephant Nature Park*, a sanctuary for abused elephants that was a little outside of Chiang Mai in the north of the country. This is where we would volunteer for a week, feeding, bathing, preparing food, shovelling poo, and giving all the love we could to these majestic animals who had been terribly abused by humans prior to their lucky rescue to this sanctuary.

I had been there the year before to celebrate my fortieth birthday and it had been one of the most awesome experiences of my life. To be amongst other dedicated animal lovers from all around the world who were choosing to live their lives a little differently gave me such inspiration.

I hadn't realised it till I was there, but part of my "sadness" at not being able to have children seemed to be highlighted daily in the life I had at home, because I was surrounded by friends who all had children. The majority of volunteers at the *Elephant Nature Park* had dedicated their lives to helping those without a voice (animals) and were not as restricted physically (and financially) as those who had families, and therefore could choose different paths, have different philosophies of life, and dedicate themselves in different ways to the world.

Anyway, on our belated long-service-leave holiday, I wanted my husband to experience all the layers of fabulousness that this volunteer experience brought, so we committed to a week together before going on to the final part of our trip, which was to include white sandy beaches and cocktails from lunchtime. We wanted to firstly get dirty, give our whole selves to these magnificent animals, and meet other like-minded humans who were doing great things in our world.

Like the year before, the experience exceeded all our expectations. We absolutely loved doing every single job we were given to support the sanctuary and to love the elephants. I could have shovelled poo all day and still have been happy doing it because I knew that it was part of the necessary chores to ensure a safe and healing environment for the elephants.

I was so pleased that my favourite elephant, Jokia, whose name means "*Eyes from Heaven*," was still around. I had a soft spot for her and had sponsored her throughout that year. During her younger days, Jokia was used in the logging trade in order to make money. When she was only two months pregnant, she went into early labour while pulling a heavy log uphill, and was not allowed to stop working to check if there was any signs of life in her still born. This event caused Jokia extreme physical and emotional trauma, and she refused to go back to work. As a result, the owners deliberately blinded her in both eyes as punishment. Once Lek (the founder of the *Elephant Nature Park*) heard about Jokia's plight, she tried on numerous occasions to buy her from the heartless owners, but couldn't afford their unreasonable asking price. Eventually though, she collaborated with another charitable group who also believed strongly in saving her. Jokia was finally rescued and has been loved and cherished ever since at the *Elephant Nature Park*.

Learning:
Self-leaders don't give up.
When they believe that something needs to be rectified, they are creative and determined to find a way.

Throughout our volunteer week, Ken was like a child in a toyshop. Not only did his big, warm, compassionate heart get to be at its best by loving the elephants, he also had a whole new audience who would listen to his stories. I mean, the man is Irish and I think was born under the blarney stone. It doesn't matter where we are, Ken always has a group around him, listening to one of his yarns and this always fills my heart and makes me smile. Twenty years into this marriage and he still makes me giggle every day. He is like an antidepressant wrapped in green. I'M SO LUCKY.

On the second last day, we walked the elephants into the jungle and stayed with them in the jungle camp. It was an incredible experience because we got to be the mahouts (the elephant carers), but without the hooks (which outside of this sanctuary is what they usually use) to walk with them up small tracks on the side of a hill until we got to our overnight destination. The jungle camp had been made as a treetop platform, so we ate, drank, slept, and watched over the elephants from high above the trees. It was incredibly serene and beautiful.

The next morning, I recall finding it hard to get out of bed, but thought that it was because the thin mattresses were not that comfortable and I was probably just tired after a week of manual labour. The walk back seemed tougher than the walk in, but again I presumed I was worn-out.

That night I still felt aches throughout my body but it was our final night at this amazing elephant sanctuary, and I wanted to enjoy a few vinos with our newfound friends, so I ignored my growing concern.

We said sad goodbyes that next morning as we began the journey to our final holiday destination – Koh Samui, a small island off the east coast of Thailand, which is renowned for its palm-fringed beaches, coconut groves, and dense, mountainous rainforests.

As I sat on the plane bracing my aching body for that short flight, I felt completely wiped out. And then the worst nightmare that can occur on a plane began. I started to get diarrhoea. Oh nooooooo. That flight was only two hours but I have to say, it was one of the longest and worst I have endured. I spent most of it locked in the bathroom, scrunched around the toilet on the floor so I could prevent 'accidents' occurring between each violent bowel movement.

Ken kept checking on me and passing through bottles of water, and apologising to the line of passengers who also needed to use the loo. I desperately wanted the flight to end and be able to curl up in a soft bed, pull the covers over my head, and let this 'bug' pass. The thought of what was to come though made me feel worse - take my seat while the plane landed, retrieve my luggage, wait patiently in a passport control line, and then endure the taxi ride to our accommodation. OMG. As I lay curled up in the foetal position in that stinky aeroplane bathroom, I thought, "Please make this end."

At this stage, we still thought it must have been something I ate, and it's not like I hadn't had bugs like this before. When I was backpacking in Egypt, I truly thought I would die one day. My friends had gone on our pre-arranged scuba-diving trip but I had stayed behind because I had felt a bit "off" that morning. That decision to stay back by myself ended up being a life-threatening decision because I was vomiting and pooing at the same time, in 50-degree heat, with no one around to help me. The heat was horrendous and when I finally stumbled into the communal showers I collapsed onto the tiles under the cold water and let everything flow out (sorry for that picture). Someone finally found me as I teetered into unconsciousness and a doctor was called to inject me with something like Imodium and hook me up to fluids.

Learning:
Self-leaders are not martyrs.
They ask for help unashamedly.

When I got off that plane in Koh Samui I realised that this was far more than food poisoning. I could barely hold myself upright and the pain rippling through by body was like nothing I had ever experienced. I could see that Ken was also pretty worried because he was so quiet. No stories, no jokes, no big smile. For an Irishman that usually means something is wrong. And there is no doubt that something was terribly wrong with me. We needed to get me to that hotel as quick as possible, get me showered and in to bed.

The fifteen-minute drive to the hotel was absolute hell. I am not sure if things have now changed, but at the time, the road was filled with potholes and it felt like I was being dragged along a rocky river bed. Every single bump, thud, stone, and pothole sent waves of pain through my entire body.

We arrived at our accommodation and the staff helped me to our villa. Not a great start showing up at a luxurious resort and having to be carried to the room, but by this stage I was too weak and in too much pain to care about anything. It felt like the bones in my neck were actually broken, that's how bad the pain was but I was hoping that once I had a shower, took some pain killers, and curled into bed that things would start to improve. How wrong I was. I continued to deteriorate so Ken called the resort manager to our room. This manager had heard of our dramatic entrance and as soon as he looked at me he went into crisis mode and insisted I get myself quick smart to the closest hospital. On arrival to that hospital I was taken into emergency and it didn't take long for them to diagnose me with dengue fever.

I don't think I had ever heard of it. Of course, I knew all about malaria. In fact, while I travelled in Uganda, my boyfriend at the time was diagnosed with it (even though we were on anti-malarial drugs) and for a week I had to inject the treatment into his thigh. Awwww. It was a great reminder why I could never have become a nurse.

Dengue fever is a mosquito-borne tropical disease caused by the dengue virus and symptoms begin three to fourteen days after infection. I had never experienced anything like the pain of dengue fever. They call it the bone-breaking virus, and I know why. If I moved my little finger, it felt like every bone in my body smashed. It was excruciating. And all they can do is give you fluids because there is still no cure (or vaccine).

The problem of course is that when you are being pumped with fluids, your bladder always needs to be emptied, and because of particular Thai beliefs, they would not touch me between my belly button and thighs, and therefore no catheter was used. This meant I had to get off the bed and walk what I ended up calling 'the walk of horrors' to the bathroom. The reason for this was that whenever I had to go to the loo it would take me over five minutes to walk fifteen metres and I would look like a zombie from Michael Jackson's Thriller film clip. I would drag myself, pull myself, and hold onto walls, chairs and TV stands – anything I could grasp - to get myself there. No one could help me because having this bone-breaking virus meant that every time someone touched me it hurt like hell. Even someone sitting on the edge of my bed would send ripples of pain from my toes through to my head - it was unbearable. Tears would run down my face every time my bladder filled because I knew what would come on this dreaded walk. Sometimes by the time I got to the loo, I was vomiting from the pain. And of course, the heaving of the vomit action would just cause more bones to break - well, the feeling of more bones breaking. It was a vicious cycle that I never thought I'd come out of.

Meanwhile, my hubby was living it up. You see, back when we were at the elephant sanctuary he was online looking for a place for us to splash out on for the last section of our belated long-service-leave holiday in Koh Samui. He found somewhere gorgeous that was within our splash-out budget, but then on the night before we were to arrive (of course, after any cancellation period cut-off), he woke at 2 am and said, *"OMG, I've got the exchange rate all messed up, I've booked five nights at two and a half times our splash-out budget"*. What? But it was out of our control and we would simply have to deal with the financial implications once we got home.

> ***Learning:***
> ***Self-leaders don't sweat the small stuff.***
> ***The consequences of mistakes can nearly***
> ***always be remedied.***

To be honest, with my grand arrival at the resort i.e. being carried in, I did not pay much attention to the surroundings, but once Ken showed me the pictures I couldn't believe my eyes. I mean, in Thailand you get incredible places for a fraction of the price that you would pay in Australia, but when you spend two and a half times your splash-out rate, you get an off-the-chart resort that you never thought you could afford. Well, we couldn't really, but there was no turning back. This would be a minor setback that we would sort out back in Australia (perhaps no pretty dresses for 12 months ☹), but now that we were booked, all we could do was enjoy it.

That seemed like a great plan to me until I had to be rushed from our villa to the hospital on that first day. Thankfully we had good travel insurance, so for the nine nights I spent in hospital, trying not to even breathe so it wouldn't feel like my bones were breaking, my gorgeous leprechaun enjoyed four extra extravagant nights for free in that amazing villa with a private butler and an infinity surround pool overlooking the ocean.

Not only that, the friends we had made at the elephant park changed their travel plans and came to Koh Samui to see us, and therefore Ken got to party with them all night, hang out with them at our villa, and pretty much have the time of his life.

Learning:
Self-leaders make the most of all opportunities ... and my hubby was definitely doing that.

Meanwhile, back at the hospital, I was suffering through the walk of horrors, bone-breaking pain, a constantly full bladder, days that lasted a lifetime, and an inability to eat. My lowest point came when I had to poo my pants while lying in bed because I couldn't bear the pain of walking to the toilet one more time that day. It was truly intolerable.

They had told me that I would know I was getting better once my hands and feet started to itch and on day eight the itch finally came. I called for the nurse to tell them and I felt excited because this meant I was finally on the mend and hopefully could soon be discharged. She gave me an antihistamine and I lay back and waited for it to kick in.

But it didn't. And my itch got worse and worse to the point of being unbearable. I called the nurse back in to ask her for something stronger and she said that unfortunately if the antihistamine didn't work then there wasn't anything else to alleviate the itch. When I asked how long it would last, thinking she would say a few hours, which of course I could deal with - just - she said that it could be three to five days. Oh nooooooo. There was no way I could stand this for three to five days. I felt like I was going insane. Bring back the bone-breaking pain. Well, I didn't really mean that, but this was another layer of horrible. It felt like there were a thousand bugs running around underneath my skin biting it constantly and if I scratched, the feeling just got worse. I thought that pre-HSC itch was horrendous, but this was something else.

This intolerable itch lasted on and off for about a week. When I finally got out of the hospital in Thailand I found myself back in again due to that damn itch. Aaaaaah. I wanted to rip off all of my skin – anything to make it stop.

After another twenty-four hours in hospital we made the decision to get back to Sydney as we had already been away so long, and although Ken was in his element living like the king of Ireland in our villa, we both had businesses to get back to.

The flight from Koh Samui through to Sydney took fifteen hours door-to-door. To say I was physically exhausted is an understatement, and when we finally arrived home ... I was done. Unfortunately the flight had taken its toll, and I relapsed that evening as I had exerted myself too much and ended up in Royal North Shore Emergency. Another bloody hospital.

Dengue fever symptoms usually last two to four weeks. It took me eighteen months to feel well again. It was a terrible time. I was so wiped out, in so much pain, and there was a constant feeling of poison running through my veins every minute of every day. I was also hypersensitive to light and sound so would need to stay in a dark, quiet room for days on end. I couldn't exercise, and for the majority of the time I couldn't go to work.

When you own and run a small business this is a MASSIVE problem. I had up to fifteen staff, hundreds of clients, and I was unable to be a leader, to be a colleague, or to be a business owner. It was a very trying time.

Reflection

Out of tough times good things grow and this setback taught me invaluable lessons on delegation, great recruitment, robust business systems and self-care.

What setbacks have you already experienced in your life?

How have they influenced you?

What have you learnt from them?

How have you transformed those setbacks into self-care?

I learnt these *Self-Leadership Strategies* from the Dengue Fever SETBACK

1. Systems and Processes

To own and run a small business, and/or to lead teams, you must have systems and processes in place, because life throws curve balls at you when you least expect it. When things come tumbling down, and you are in the middle of a major setback, you often don't have the time or energy or resources to do much about it. If you haven't already put procedures in place, then life can very quickly spiral out of control.

From day dot, you must ask yourself what would be the worst-case scenario? For me, this ended up being my inability to show up for work but still wanting to provide jobs, mortgage repayments, and purpose to everyone who worked for me. This became a very compelling motivator to get every last tiny procedure written down so the instructions could be consistently followed, and the business could continue to be viable.

If you knew this was going to happen, what would you have to do today to ensure you'd survive? Spend ten minutes a day writing out processes that others can stick to, so the work can be continued when you are not there. I have always collated my processes into what I call the Red Bus Book. If a big red bus hits me then everything is written down for someone else to successfully follow. When the details are documented efficiency improves, errors are reduced, and there is a go-to-place for instructions on all the business components. This results in improved productivity, probable scalability, and a healthier profitability.

2. Surround Yourself With The Right People

If I didn't have the team I had around me on my return from Thailand, there is no way my business would have survived. Fortunately, I had already worked hard on the processes, but processes alone will not mean your business can survive. I am proud to say that I had spent years genuinely building trust and nurturing relationships, which meant at crunch time, the people around me - staff, suppliers, stakeholders - were willing to step up and support me throughout this setback.

Cultivating goodwill takes time and it has to be authentic. There needs to be a mutual respect and you won't get that if you haven't chosen the right people for your team in the first place.

3. SELF-CARE

This was my greatest learning from the dengue fever setback. My healing did not go to plan. It took eighteen months rather than the expected two to four weeks. I had to give in to this and create a new timeline and thought process for my life. Complete rest is not something I was familiar with or comfortable with, but I soon learnt that if I overdid it then I would feel the ramifications for days, if not weeks.

Learning to slow everything down is incredibly hard when you have always been a go-getter. Paying attention to what my brain and body were telling me became my daily goal. In the past I would ignore the signs and symptoms of anything my body was trying to tell me because the fact was, I did not have the time or inclination to be in second gear.

To experience this dengue fever setback has actually allowed me to extract such powerful lessons about self-care. Not just for me, but also for the individuals, teams, and companies that I would work with in the upcoming decades.

To rest and rejuvenate is a piece that nearly all busy professionals struggle with. I mean, who has the time when our "to do" lists are so long?

What I have learnt though from my own personal experiences and from what I see during my workshops, is that the inability to take time out … even five minutes a day … can very quickly lead you from merely surviving with all the responsibilities, stressors, and challenges of life, to actually burning out.

And a lot of people don't come back from burnout.

It takes courage to put your health and wellbeing first in a world that admires people who proudly declare that they've been awake all night to finish a report, or are so important that they have to work through lunch every day, or who have spent their family holidays replying to emails.

Self-leaders know if they can't lead themselves, then they can't expect to lead others and this has to start with self-care.

Closing Chapter Reminder

Setbacks can eventually teach us the benefits of self-care once we draw on the positive insights gained from our adversities.

When we courageously embrace the powers of self-leadership and habitually take action in a way that is right for our lives, we can step up and create real and sustainable change.

Over time this means that together, as resilient, optimistic and inspired self-leaders we can make the most impactful difference to our lives, to our workplaces, to our communities, and to our world.

Chapter Eight

Chaos into CLARITY

"Someone's sitting in the shade today because someone planted a tree a long time ago."

Warren Buffett

It was the 12th of March, 2015, and a momentous event had occurred. I sold my business, *Jump Start Your Life*, which I had created seventeen years ago from my stinky garage with two hundred dollars' worth of second-hand equipment from Cash Converters.

Learning:
Self-leaders don't let their humble beginnings
or their surroundings deter them
from achieving their dreams.

No more 5am starts with 9pm finishes. Woohoo. No more getting up in the middle of winter on a wet and cold morning trying to work out how we were going to fit everyone in the studio because it was pouring rain and the clients liked being outdoors and there wasn't enough room for them all. Woohoo. No more worrying about having enough clients to make sure my incredible staff had enough hours to keep them financially viable. Woohoo. I have to tell you, I was one happy ex-business owner … well, at least for a little while.

As I sat in our local Spanish restaurant with my husband, sister, and friend, drinking champagne to celebrate the sale of that business, I watched in horror the chaos that was heading full steam ahead to my beloved Vanuatu. A place that had been my second home since I was twenty years of age.

Cyclone Pam was gaining momentum and its two hundred and fifty kilometre winds were about to hit this beautiful island nation within the next forty-eight hours. Unfortunately instead of celebrating in style, all I could think about was this cyclone and I was constantly peeking at my phone under the table for updates, hoping against all odds that the reports were wrong. But unfortunately they weren't.

Focusing on that celebration dinner was incredibly difficult, knowing what all my friends in Vanuatu were about to endure. Once we came home, I called as many as I could to find out what they were doing to prepare for it and if there was anything I could do to help from Sydney. Of course, there wasn't. All I could do was send my thoughts and love to them. It was a terrible feeling of having no control. Mother Nature was on her way to reap absolute havoc to these defenceless islands, homes and people … and she did.

Cyclone Pam was the greatest natural disaster that Vanuatu had ever seen. The destruction it caused was catastrophic and the implications for the people and the country were shattering. Seventy-five thousand people were left homeless because of the fury of that storm, which ripped apart the thatched hut homes that they lived in, it destroyed the country's delicate infrastructure, drastically impacted the ability of thousands to earn money, and it tragically killed sixteen people.

I did not sleep a wink that night as I was glued to my cyclone app and continually tried to call my friends, but of course, all communication had stopped. The cyclone had arrived and I felt absolutely helpless as my mind feared the worst.

As the next thirty-six hours unfolded we saw the devastation that the cyclone had inflicted on Port Vila. It was heart-breaking as the destruction was beyond anything I could have imagined and the footage that was coming out through the media outlets showed that Port Vila was ruined. From all my times visiting this beautiful nation, I knew that the most robust of Vanuatu's buildings were to be found in the capital, so if they had been ruined, this meant that the remainder of the country who were in grass huts would experience a far worse fate.

Tanna, an island south of Efate, which is only forty kilometres long and nineteen kilometres wide, was still to be hit with the eye of the cyclone and I couldn't even begin to imagine how they would survive the impending ferocity.

I had spent so much time on Tanna over the years because it was where *Jump Start Foundation* had done our most impactful work with education and sport sponsorships, girls' empowerment workshops, and of course, our greatest achievement of all, building the library. I was so scared for all my friends who lived in this quiet, peaceful corner of the world, knowing that they were in serious danger. Mother Nature was on her way, and nothing was going to stop her.

For five days after this category five cyclone (the worst of all the categories) had hit the island of Tanna we had no contact with our friends or the community that we had worked with over the last ten years. In fact, because all the communication towers were destroyed, no one was able to find out how the people were. All we knew was that Cyclone Pam's fury had hit this tiny island with all its might, and we couldn't help but wonder how on earth they could survive such intensity when they only had small, fragile shelters to keep them safe.

The first satellite images came out on the 20th March, six days after the eye of the storm had torn through Tanna. I could not believe what I was looking at. The island had been obliterated and so had all the impactful work that we had done over the last ten years. This of course was heartbreaking but I knew that a library could be rebuilt, books could be replaced, teaching aids could again be supplied, and the required literacy resources shipped over. The lives of the people was what I was most worried about.

Learning:
Self-leaders can quickly prioritise what is most urgent for their focus and what the next most important step is.

The people on Tanna are subsistence farmers, which means they eat what they grow. Unfortunately, Cyclone Pam had obliterated ninety percent of their food supply, and aid organisations were saying if they didn't get food to the island soon, they would all starve. I'll never forget the feeling of complete despair when I read this, and bursting into tears in my office. By this stage, the clients had stopped asking me if I had heard anything because the look on my face told it all. I couldn't sleep or eat or think about anything else apart from how they were all coping.

Thankfully the next day I received a phone call from Hugh, who owns Tanna Lodge, the accommodation we always stayed at, to say that the place was a complete mess but in their area there had been no lives lost. It was an absolute miracle. And one that I would not be able to fully grasp until I arrived and saw with my own eyes the depth of the damage that had taken place.

Mother Nature was angry, but she had spared lives, and for that I will be forever grateful.

The stories of how they all survived were incredible. One of the elders told me that in their village, they made all the children curl up together on the ground, the mamas knelt over them, and the papas then lay across them all, linking arms to keep everyone safe. They stayed this way for three to four hours while the cyclone wreaked havoc above them.

Learning:
Self-leaders are resourceful.
They find solutions in places others wouldn't think to look.

The people of Vanuatu are ingenious and resilient, and they did whatever they could to keep their families safe. In one sense, the fact that their homes were made from natural products meant that when the cyclone ripped their homes apart, the materials that were flying around the village were not tiles or bricks or steel that would instantly kill them. So even though branches and leaves and palm fronds don't protect you in one way, they in fact protect you in this scenario.

I knew from the moment I first saw Cyclone Pam on my phone in that restaurant the night I sold my business, that I was going to have to get myself to Vanuatu to do whatever I could. No matter how small that might be. I was finally able to get a flight to Vanuatu thirteen days after the cyclone hit. Every time I had been on that Sydney to Vila flight over the past fifteen years, it was always such a happy, exciting time. This flight though was so different, as everyone felt sadness and apprehension about what we would physically see with our own eyes once we landed.

Looking out the window as we flew into Port Vila, all I could see were thousands of coconut palms wrenched out of the ground at the roots and scattered everywhere. It reminded me of that game called Fiddle Sticks that we used to play as kids. You would have a bunch of thin sticks that you let fall down onto the table and then the game would start. All of these broken palm trees looked like a gigantic game of Fiddle Sticks.

As we walked across the tarmac from the plane, there was a feeling of eeriness to the atmosphere and people were openly crying. It's impossible to grasp the magnitude of what has occurred from the TV, but once I was on the ground, I could comprehend the full power of that cyclone, and it made me feel helpless.

The flight I was on was one of the first to arrive into the country after the airport was finally reopened. The whole country had been declared a natural disaster zone and an international relief effort was put in place. It was an absolute logistical nightmare to reach everyone who had been impacted due to the fact they were spread across the eighty three islands that made up the archipelago of Vanuatu. The Armed Forces from Australia, New Zealand, and New Caledonia were sent and they were doing their best to restore the essential elements that human beings need to survive – food, water, sanitation and shelter.

I only wanted to stay one night in Vila because I desperately needed to get to Tanna so I could understand how I could best support our community in whatever way they needed. I had thought Port Vila was bad, but nothing could have prepared me for Tanna. It was like something out of a movie. A disaster movie. Actually, more like a war movie because not only did it seem that this tropical jungle oasis had been flattened with no trees left standing, but there were army tanks and helicopters and hundreds of people from the armed forces from around the world, and at least a dozen different aid organisations.

My friend Regina from Port Vila came with me to Tanna for moral support. She knew (more than me) how hard it was going to be to see over ten years of hard work ruined and wanted to be my right-hand gal. I was very grateful for this.

Learning:
Self-leaders accept the kind hand that is held out to them in times of trouble.

Hugh picked us up from the airport and took us straight to the school so we could assess the damage and let our community know that we were there to help pick up the pieces - physically and emotionally. They had all lost so much - their homes, their food supply, their clean water source, their education facilities, and their possessions.

It was devastating.

To see with my own eyes the destruction that had been caused was overwhelming. It was hard to believe that only eight months prior I had been here with my husband, my sister, my godmother, my close family friends, and my wonderfully compassionate *Jump Start Foundation* supporters for one of the most important days of my life.

We had had the most exhilarating and fulfilling day with the official opening of the library. There had been traditional dancers, heartfelt speeches, Melanesian feasts, a stampede to be the first through the newly opened library, and stories read to young and old from the beautiful, brand-new culturally appropriate books that we had all worked so hard to afford.

Now it was all ruined. The roof was gone, the windows smashed, and the books scattered into piles of soggy paper. The principal, Jackson, and his wife, Doreen, were there to greet me and we all hugged and cried together at the sight of this ruined project.

Miraculously though, no one in the community that we had built this library for had lost their lives, which we were so grateful for. In fact, I was surprised that the overall death toll across the country was incredibly low considering the ferociousness of the cyclone, but of course, even one life lost is one too many.

There was no time, nor purpose, to feel sorry for ourselves though, because no one could wave a magic wand to turn this chaos around;

we had to roll up our sleeves and get ourselves dirty. I knew that I would not be able to make a difference on a big scale because I did not have the resources or skills to help everyone, all I could do is help our school get back on their feet. After long discussions with the principal and the teachers, we decided that we would make it our goal to get the school up and running as soon as we could.

> *"The universe doesn't give you*
> *what you ask for with your thoughts;*
> *it gives you what you demand*
> *with your actions."*
> Dr. Steve Maraboli

To achieve this, we needed to encourage the children to come back to school, despite being unable to conduct normal classes ... yet. The message was sent out that we needed helpers to clean up the mess so everyone could get back to a routine as quickly as possible.

The challenges of course were that food and water supplies were very low and some children had a long way to walk, but I was amazed that the next day we had over one hundred smiling, enthusiastic children ready and waiting to work at cleaning up their school.

Learning:
Self-leaders of the future never take for granted the opportunities they get to improve their education.

That amazing Vanuatu nature of being happy to help in any way they could, brought me to tears. Here they were, after the worst cyclone to ever have hit the country, yet instead of feeling sorry for themselves, they showed up eager to lend a helping hand.

We all rolled up our sleeves and got stuck into the job of cleaning up the mess. I was absolutely determined that we were going to get this done. Luckily, one of my friends had suggested that I bring over water purification kits as they knew that contaminated water could quickly spread disease, and if this happened on a small island like Tanna it would not be long before an epidemic followed. I was able to bring eight over with me in my luggage, which meant that all the students and teachers (over two hundred individuals) could be assured that they were hydrated with safe drinking water. And once we cleaned up the water tank that we had installed at the school the year before, everyone from the wider community was able to access clean drinking water. What a massive difference this made. Yah ☺

During the road to recovery we found fifty books that we were able to salvage from the thousands that we had initially donated. I remember smiling to myself thinking that fifty books was more than they had a year ago so we should feel happy about that. I felt that it was up to me to keep thinking positively like this for their sakes, as they had all lost so much. We also had recruited a small team of children to search for coconuts, and it was not long before we had an abundant pile that we could all enjoy for morning tea.

After the third day of working from practically dawn to dusk, I started to worry that we had possibly bitten off more than we could chew, and the enormity of what was ahead hit me hard. This was going to take weeks... possibly months, of hard, backbreaking work with little to no tools, materials or skills. All we had was sheer willpower to improve the situation and a resolution to stay positive.

The classrooms were destroyed. All the chairs and desks were either missing legs or completely smashed. We actually found chairs and desks three hundred metres from the school as they had obviously been whooshed away in the two hundred and fifty kilometre winds. It was not until we found the colorbond roof from the library tangled in the debris more than half a kilometre away that it really hit home how fierce this cyclone had been. Again, I was shocked that no one had been killed in this area.

The children helped lift the metal roof back to the school piece by piece as we knew that we would be able to re-use it somehow, someway. It was heartbreaking to see our landmark library scattered across the countryside after there had been such a mammoth amount of effort from everyone for so long. Fundraising for that roof had been no easy task and now it was broken into a dozen pieces. I kept saying to myself, *"Come on Heidi, stay positive."*

While I was trudging up the hill the next morning to start another day of clean up, my body reminded me of the toll that this whole situation was causing. I was exhausted – physically and emotionally. The work had been relentless, I was stressed out and not sleeping, and I had no idea how we were going to raise enough money quickly enough to rebuild. Everyone was telling me to just let it go as there was no way we would be able to start over, but I didn't want to let the community down, and I was constantly doing my best to stay bright and sparkly to everyone at our school. As I wearily stepped into the school grounds, egging myself on to smile widely at all the eager little faces waiting for my direction, I was astounded to see army trucks and half a dozen army men walking around regarding the damage. It was the Australian Defence Force (ADF).

You see, the day before I had gone up to their camp to introduce myself (as a fellow Aussie) to see if they had any spare materials or tools that we could use. There was only so much we could do at the school with the salvaged resources that we had. They were curious about why I was asking, so I told them about our wonderful Isangel Central Primary School community and of our recent plight. We were in no more difficulty than any other community in Vanuatu and it had not occurred to me that they would reach out to help us in any shape or form.

The ADF were astounded by our story and what we had achieved as pure volunteers over the years, and wanted to see it with their own eyes. The fact that a Sydney girl (me) had had an aspiration to create something so valuable to the community, and had not only achieved it, but had come back to help when the country needed it the most, touched a nerve with them. And this is why they had turned up to help us. OMG. This kind gesture from the ADF overwhelmed me and I felt a surge of relief and motivation now that I had some extra talented help. I started to think that perhaps we would actually make this happen and be able to reach the goal we had set, which was to get the kids back on their education journey. Finally there was light at the end of the tunnel.

After initial chats about what we had planned, they committed to putting a roof back on our dilapidated library so the children would have somewhere for their classes until the remaining classrooms were rebuilt. I couldn't believe it.

The work the ADF did over the next six days was nothing short of a miracle. They drilled, lifted, nailed, screwed, cut, hammered, worked and sweated from dawn to dust until they turned a scene of devastation into a school again. The crowning moment was when they put a new roof back on our library. We knew it would not be used as a library for quite a while, but at least it was a safe place where the children could gather and be taught their lessons. That afternoon I cried tears of joy as I knew that if it wasn't for the ADF it would probably have been eighteen months before anything was done because the logistics of getting building materials to Tanna was now close to impossible. The reality was that to have these knights in shining armour there, with all the necessary materials, to generously focus on our needs, was a miracle.

How on earth could we get this lucky?

Learning:
Sometimes the universe brings unexpected generosity to self-leaders who have done good deeds.

Oh my, the joy this brought to so many. It felt like it was all going to be okay. Lady Luck would keep coming our way and we would get through the chaos that Cyclone Pam had thrown at us. To have the manpower and know-how of these generous human beings who had dedicated their lives to helping others in times of trouble gave us such a boost. You could actually feel the heaviness lift off everyone in the surrounding villages because they knew that there were people around the world who were willing to support them as they got back on their feet.

As I continued to drag never-ending bags of debris out of the school, my heart lifted and the fire in my belly was again reignited.

One morning I arrived a little later because I was drafting some correspondence to send back to Australia to all our supporters. Rumour was that that afternoon, a communication tent would be set up for us in Lenakel (the main town of the island) and the internet would finally be available. Woohoo. On arrival to the school, all the ADF men were sitting around under the trees looking sheepish, which was very unlike them.

They were embarrassed to tell me that they were not allowed to work anymore until they got an all-clear because a caterpillar had bitten one of their men on his finger and due to the fact that there was only one ADF medic on Tanna, all of them had to stop work until this situation was sorted, because they couldn't risk another man being "injured".

I couldn't really grasp what they were telling me. I mean, did you say a caterpillar had bitten him on his finger? Surely this was not critical enough for everyone on the island to stop work?

Apparently though, this was the rule, because if they kept working and a different ADF member was injured, the medic could not be in two places at once, hence why the rule had to be in place.

Seriously? This cracked me up. I mean, we are surrounded by devastation, people didn't have enough food, shelter, or water, and because one man has a caterpillar bite on his finger then we all need to sit around. Crazy.

Learning:
***Self-leadership comes in many shapes and sizes.
There was no doubt in my mind that these men
had many self-leadership qualities but they also had to
stick to the rules ... even the ones that seemed quite odd.***

The caterpillar story did not end up being the main story for the day because as promised the communication tent had been set up by one of the International Telco NGO's and I was headed straight for it.

I knew that everyone at home would be patiently waiting for news from me, so I was speed typing as much information as I could. It's a funny thing when you have not had any contact with the outside world for days and then you have it again. It's like a drug that you can't get enough of. I wanted to let them know how excited and proud I was. Excited because I could tell them that relief was finally coming through to the islands, and that we had the backing of the Australian Defence Force who were working tirelessly to support us.

I also wanted to let them know how proud I was of their big, generous hearts. It had been less than three weeks since I had reached out to our supporters about the consequences that Cyclone Pam had caused, and to my absolute shock over one hundred thousand dollars had been donated to us. Amazing. Amazing. Amazing. Methodist Ladies College in Melbourne who had partnered with us for the last couple of years, were substantially amazing. They held a fundraiser with the goal of raising ten thousand dollars in ten minutes but due to incredible supporters, such as Melissa L, who galvanised the entire school into action, they ended up handing over twenty-seven thousand dollars to us. *Oh my.*

As I was reeling in this moment of bliss from the enormous amount of support that was coming in, I heard a man speaking outside through what sounded like a handheld megaphone. He was speaking in Bislama (Vanuatu's local language), which I could understand a little bit of, but not enough to get the essence of, so I ignored it. In any case, I was too focused on getting news back home to our stakeholders.

Five minutes later, I heard it again, but this time I could hear panic in his tone so I looked around the tent and noticed that everyone except for a local lady sitting opposite me had gone. I said to her, *"Hey, where's everyone gone? What's going on? What is that guy saying?"* she said, *"Oh,"* in a very relaxed island-time voice. *"There's a tsunami coming."*

"A tsunami?" I said. *"Okay. Where to?"* She said, *"Here, to Tanna."* I'm like, *"When is this tsunami coming?"* She said, *"2:34pm"* I looked at my laptop, and it was 2:21pm. YIKES. I scooped up my belongings and ran outside of the tent. Much to my horror, everyone was sprinting.

There was absolute mayhem going on, because the vast Pacific was only about thirty metres away and therefore everyone was heading for the hills. Mamas were carrying their crying babies, papas were dragging their reluctant children, and everyone was pushing and shoving to get into the few available vehicles so they could make a quick getaway and get to high ground.

I was freaking out.

Now, I am not sure if you have seen the movie *The Impossible* with Naomi Watts? It's a re-enactment of the horrific Boxing Day tsunami. She's sitting leisurely by the pool with her family before the tsunami arrived, and right up to the moment before it hit, the water looks completely calm. And so right in this moment on Tanna, I am looking out at the calm Pacific in front of me, remembering that movie, thinking, it doesn't matter that it looks this calm, because it's about to be a ginormous life-threatening wave, and I could be about to die.

In the middle of my freak-out, a UNICEF vehicle screeched to a halt right next to me and shrieked, *"Get in the ute. Get in the ute."* I jumped into the back of the ute with them, and they drove up the hill. I'm thinking, *Oh my gosh. I could actually be about to die.* I better call my husband.

Ring, ring. Ring, ring. Ken didn't pick up and the damn thing said to me, "The person you are trying to reach is unavailable, please leave your message and this will be converted to a text."

You have got to be joking. Telstra. I hate you. This could be the last time I ever get to speak with him and it goes to voice-to-text. I couldn't believe it.

But I did my best to speak clearly, with children screaming and the suspension of the ute screeching … *"Darling, there's a tsunami coming and I don't know when I'm going to get to talk to you again, but I want you to know that I…"* And before I could complete my sentence and say "… *love you,"* Telstra says back to me, "Thank you for your message, it will be converted to a text."

Nooooooooooooooooooo.

Of course, here I sit writing this book so it is obvious that I am alive and well. Thankfully, the tsunami broke one hundred metres offshore, and we all lived another day. Mother Nature had decided at the eleventh hour that she had reaped enough damage to this small island nation, which I will be eternally grateful for.

When I finally got through to my hubby, he said that the translation to text was all gobbledygook and he couldn't understand a word of it, so lucky it wasn't my last love message to him ♥

Reflection

The chaos caused by a catastrophic cyclone and a terminated tsunami has taught me self-leadership strategies on many things in my life, including how to go back to the foundations, the benefits of sitting in silence, and how to get crystal clear clarity when things seem overwhelmingly difficult.

What are the chaotic experiences you have already had in your life?

How have they influenced you?

What have you learnt from them?

How have you transformed this chaos into clarity?

I learnt these three
Self-Leadership Strategies
from the
Cyclone Pam CHAOS

1. Foundations First

When things in a workplace are not going to plan; when you are not even close to reaching financial goals; when you are having to constantly solve problems rather than working on the strategy; and when your best staff are being headhunted by the competition, go back to your foundations.

When there is a crisis, it is very easy to focus on the wrong thing.

If you have ever been taught first aid, you will remember the DRABC sequence - danger, response, airway, breathing, circulation. There is no point worrying about and patching a bleeding arm, even though a lot of blood draws your attention to it. You must first check that you and all those around you are not in danger.

You have to go back to the foundations. What is your goal? What is your purpose? Why are you doing what you are doing? Who should you surround yourself with? Why them? What is the one thing you can do next to gain the most positive result?

As a self-leader you learn how to recognise what the very next step must be even when louder, brighter steps are fighting for your attention.

2. Sitting in Silence

During the time when we had no idea whether the people in our community on Tanna were dead or alive, I felt the full brunt of physical and emotional anxiety and stress. I wasn't sleeping, I didn't care about the risks I would put myself in by going to a disaster zone, I was racing around on adrenaline, making silly mistakes, and at times I felt like I could hardly breathe.

This is when I learnt that the breath is the only known method that can successfully interrupt the stress response. When you breathe deep into your tummy, you involuntarily slow down your automatic fight or flight reaction, which has calming effects on your mind and body.

When you are under a lot of pressure at work and things are overwhelming and you can't see an end in sight, find a way to sit without distraction for five minutes and concentrate on your breathing.

Sitting still, away from the stresses of your life, and focusing on taking slow, deep breaths can work miracles for your ability to deal with upcoming obstacles.

Over the years I have tried to sit and meditate knowing the benefits that it will bring to my busy mind, but I often hit roadblocks because my brain says, *"Yah, you have finally sat down so now we can go through our to-do lists for the rest of the day."*

I find I have much more success if I say I am sitting in silence with all my devices turned off or in another room. That way, when my mind wanders, I don't beat myself up because in fact I am still reaping the benefits of sitting still in silence and concentrating on my breathing.

If you have also had trouble meditating in the traditional sense, perhaps it's worth reframing it like I do and dedicating five minutes a day to sitting in silence.

3. CLARITY

Being able to cut through the noise during chaotic times is a powerful skill. Being able to have razor-sharp clarity on what to prioritise next will allow you to become the talented leader everyone aspires to being.

The Cyclone Pam situation helped me to formulate a clear framework on how to quickly come down to the most important next step that would have the greatest impact.

At the time, this was to create an environment where children could gain some routine back to their life after having gone through such a traumatic natural disaster. It was clear we needed to get them back to school, where they could be physically safe, mentally stimulated and holistically nurtured. I am extremely proud to say we were the first school on Tanna after the cyclone to be up and running.

The simple, yet effective framework that I used was one I had been working on during times in my life when I was juggling far too many balls, but the chaos of Cyclone Pam was the first time I was able to apply it on a bigger scale.

I now call this my *Glass Jar Framework* and I use it to successfully educate leaders and their teams on how to discover what is the most impactful thing they need to do next during difficult situations, which will have the most positive bearing on them and all those around them. It results in being able to untangle complex problems and get crystal clear clarity of the one thing that is right for that specific situation.

The beauty of this Glass Jar methodology is that it is straightforward, uncomplicated and can be easily applied to various scenarios. It is one of the most impactful strategies that I teach in my Courageous Self-Leadership Masterclass that you can read about in the upcoming chapter called *Next Steps*.

Closing Chapter Reminder

Enduring chaotic situations can help us to gain real clarity once we draw on the positive insights gained from our adversities.

When we courageously embrace the powers of self-leadership and habitually take action in a way that is right for our lives, we can step up and create real and sustainable change.

Over time this means that together, as resilient, optimistic and inspired self-leaders we can make the most impactful difference to our lives, to our workplaces, to our communities, and to our world.

Chapter Nine

The Resilience Bucket

> *"You are not born with a fixed amount of resilience. Like a muscle, you can build it up and draw on it when you need it. In that process you will figure out who you really are – and you just might become the very best version of yourself."*
>
> Sheryl Sandberg

All of us have our own individual levels of resilience.

Some of us start with a solid, hardwearing bucket made of steel.

Some of us start with a fragile, vulnerable bucket made of straw.

It differs for many reasons and our capacity to be resilient changes throughout our lifetimes. Sometimes our resilience bucket is strong and impenetrable, but other times it is weaker and has many leaks.

Whatever our starting point, we all have the ability to influence our buckets and either keep them sturdy or make them unsteady.

Self-Leader Warning Signs

As a self-leader you have to constantly maintain your bucket, because it is nearly impossible to be impactful when you have a bucket with holes. You can try and plug the leaks with Band-Aid solutions (such as alcohol, food, prescription medication, or online shopping.) but in the end, the adhesive wears off, and the leaks keep on oozing, and they get harder to patch.

When you deplete your resilience bucket, it's like a festering wound that has not been treated from the inside out with antibiotics. It becomes red, sore, ugly, full of pus, and no amount of Band-Aids make a difference.

Your brain and body does speak on behalf of your bucket to let you know when it's running on empty. It sends out warning signals but unfortunately due to this hectic, noisy 24/7 world we live in, it is hard to hear the messages.

When we ignore the warning signs that our buckets are low on resources because of all the leaks, then we put our physical and mental health in jeopardy.

These are some of the **physical ill-health warning signs** that can occur when your bucket is depleted:

- Cold sores
- Headaches
- Constipation, bloating
- Weight gain or weight loss
- Muscle pain
- Lengthy colds and flus
- Poor performing immune system

These are some of the **mental ill-health warning signs** that can occur when your bucket is depleted:

- Anger
- Sarcasm
- Memory loss, poor decisions, mistakes
- Insomnia
- Withdrawal from family, friends, hobbies
- Stress
- Burnout
- Anxiety
- Depression

These are some of the **behavioural warning signs** that can occur when your bucket is depleted:

- You submit an important report that is filled with errors.
- You snap at your children for no real reason after a long day at work.
- You cause a fight with your partner that has created chaos in your home.
- You start to hibernate and refrain from attending social events that you used to love.
- You consume unhealthy quantities of food and alcohol.

There is no doubt, especially when you are a self-leader, that it is hard to pay attention to these signs when so many people and projects are demanding your attention. How on earth are you expected to hear subtle messages when everyone else is shouting so loudly? When you learn to listen to these faint yet powerful expressions of caution, it allows you to make educated decisions, even under intense pressure.

When you don't listen, it's like you are allowing a big power drill to penetrate your bucket while you have your back turned, so that all the resources you have been carefully storing start pouring out.

Find out how full your Resilience Bucket is by taking the two-minute quiz at www.HeidiDening.com

Don't Deplete Your Bucket

When you deplete your resilience bucket of it's resources, you put yourself at risk of being unable to deal with life's curve balls. The big and the small ones. In your professional life and your personal life.

In the following chapter, I will be sharing with you a story that caused me so much rage, so much trauma, and so much loss. I'm fully aware that compared to some war-torn places of the world, this incident might not even hit the Richter scale, but in my life, it was shattering and it came very close to breaking me.

On reflection though, my break was close, not only because it was such a traumatic event, but also because my bucket by that stage, was so depleted that I had no resources left to crawl out of the deep, dark hole where I had fallen.

As a self-leader, it's important to realise that you can keep going and going and slap on the Band-Aid and tell everyone you are okay, but if that bucket of yours has holes in it, then you are in danger of hurting yourself and everyone around you.

It is incredibly important for me to teach this lesson. I've learnt it the hard way, and if I can prevent one more person from being negatively impacted by their depleted bucket then I know that it will have been worthwhile.

Because, you see, prior to having petrol bombs thrown at my bedroom (which I write about in the next chapter *Rage into Resilience*), I had chosen to ignore the impacts of some other fairly momentous experiences.

For thirteen years, my sister, my husband, and I had been caring for my terminally ill parents in the family home where we had grown up. When my dad died, I truthfully thought I would never smile again. He had always been my superhero. He died when his bowel cancer travelled to his lungs, his bones, and his brain. Nine months after he died, my mum was diagnosed with bowel cancer that travelled to her lungs, her bones, and her brain and after eight years of putting up an incredible fight that would have put Muhammad Ali to shame, we also lost her to this despicable disease.

Grief puts massive holes in your bucket, especially when it has worn you down as much as the years of this caretaking of my parents had caused.

Not only was my bucket depleted from my intense grief, but also only ten months prior to the petrol bombs, a friend's father silently crept into my closed bedroom without permission and behaved indecently while I slept at her place. Due to the overwhelming impact that this incident had not only on me, but also on my friend and her relationship with her father, I chose to push this deep inside me.

I hope you can understand to protect my friend I don't want to discuss the details about this incident, as she also has had to deal with the deep betrayal and disgust that her father caused both of us, and writing the details here won't serve anybody. All I want to write about is my eventual acknowledgment of what it triggered and how I have learnt more about my resilience bucket because of this.

I've learnt that when you ignore anger, grief, pain, trauma and betrayal your bucket starts to rot from the inside out. It weakens the whole composition of your vessel, of your life, and so when the next knock thumps on the outside, even from the smallest of incidents, breakdown occurs.

My mistake had been that I had allowed my bucket to become extremely depleted of all its resources. Grief from losing my parents, emotional pain caused by my friend's father, and physical pain from a car accident that caused severe whiplash, had all taken their toll on my mind and body.

As a self-leader what are you doing to check that your resources are not diminishing to a point of break down? Who are you listening to? Do you require a trusted advisor to let you know when it's essential for you to recharge because you hardly ever prioritise yourself? Be honest and reach out to someone who you know will look for these warning signs and gently direct you when you are too depleted to direct yourself.

I know with absolute certainty that I will never allow myself to get to that level of depletion again, because we never know what life is about to throw at us. If our bucket is already running on empty and then something "big" happens, it's very hard to bounce back from it.

As a better self-leader I now know when to say "no."

I now know when to switch off my devices, get more sleep, move my body, read a book, feel the sun on my back, connect with loved ones, and nourish myself with good food.

I know the daily habits I need to be obsessive about to ensure I have the necessary resources at all times to be the best self-leader I can be. The best wife, sister, colleague, friend, godmother, and aunt.

It has not been easy to evolve into this understanding of what I need and to know that it is completely OK to give myself permission to put myself first. But I'm now reaping the rewards of those life-changing lessons.

How To Strengthen Your Bucket

The repetition of small daily actions during your good times is what can hold you together during times of struggle. The monotonous acts that are often hard, boring and relentless are what can support you when you need it most.

Recognising what works for you is crucial if your bucket lining is to harden and keep you steady. Knowing what must take priority takes a lot of self-awareness but it allows you to have clarity, direction and structure in your day, your week, and your life when things are not going to plan.

PERSONAL

Resilience Bucket

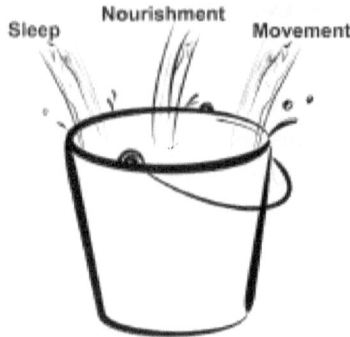

To proactively improve the strength of your personal Resilience Bucket you could start with these three important bucket-fillers.

1. **Sleep** – getting enough sleep is the elixir of life. It gives you brain-power, energy, clarity and an ability to step up and reach for the stars.

   Unfortunately though, when we are stressed it is difficult to fall asleep and stay asleep. If we wake up the next day sleep-deprived it becomes a struggle to deal with the day's requirements.

   There are a couple of times in my life when I have had crippling insomnia, and have had to retrain my brain and body to fall asleep and stay asleep. For a proven method that has worked for me and so many others, please email me at heidi@heididening.com

   Getting a good night sleep strengthens buckets, so do whatever you can to make this happen.

2. **Movement** – moving your body helps your muscles to relax and it increases blood flow. This improves energy levels and

our ability to focus. It also encourages the release of endorphins (which I call nature's happy pills), providing a sense of calmness and a positive outlook on life. All these factors help to build steel linings in resilience buckets.

The benefits of moving more are hard to appreciate until you actually experience it and then feel the positive impact that it has on your ability to cope.

Personally, if I don't move daily, even if it is just a short, simple stretching sequence on my lounge room floor, then I struggle to be as decisive as I should be, I struggle to get things done in a reasonable amount of time, and I struggle to handle stressful situations, conversations and projects.

How can you add a little more movement to your day so you can strengthen your bucket?

3. **Nourishment** – food forms the basis of our physical and mental performance. If you upgrade what you consume, you upgrade your mental clarity, decision-making ability, energy levels and resilience bucket.

If you nourish yourself with an abundance of natural food that comes primarily from mother nature, it will have a positive impact on your brain and body.

On the flip-side, if you consume artificial food that comes out of a packet and it has numbers or words that you don't understand on the ingredients list, then you will start to rot your body and your resilience bucket from the inside out.

Ill-health impacts our ability to cope with life's unexpected surprises.

Other personal bucket fillers could be the inclusion of hobbies, time spent in nature, connection to friends and family, and/or volunteering for a cause you feel passionate about.

The Resilience Bucket At Work

The Resilience Bucket concept also works at an organisational level.

If a work environment is toxic, if people are expected to work unreasonable hours, if no one gets to leave their desk for meals, if there is an expectation to be "on" for twenty-four hours a day, if they have to take calls while eating dinner with their families, if while on holidays they are required to reply to emails, etc. etc., then their buckets will start to weaken.

If this becomes the "norm," then the organisation is at risk. When a workplace creates holes in the buckets of their people, problems escalate as resources start to spill out.

First you will notice that everyone is starting to bicker with each other, productivity will decrease, office politics will start, absenteeism will rise, mistakes will be made, profits will be down, and your best staff will leave.

The organisations that have not already created a thriving work culture find it difficult to recognise when their company buckets are low on resources. The reason for this is that they are so frantic patching holes and so blinded fighting fires, that they don't recognise the warning signs.

Workplaces should be particularly motivated to provide the capability for their people to keep their buckets full.

This can be accomplished by educating everyone at all levels of the organisation about what elements can be added to the bucket to keep it robust, and at the same time, understand and acknowledge what elements will deplete its natural state. When staff buckets are running on empty, two of the main repercussions is an increase in absenteeism and presenteeism and the cost of this to Australian workplaces is upwards of thirty-five billion dollars a year.

When I work with leaders and their teams during my workshop programs, I am easily able to recognise the signs of depleted workplace buckets. When the culture is rotting from the inside out, it creates big gaping holes in their company bucket and good opportunities, hard-earned dollars, and great people start spilling out.

WORKPLACE

Resilience Bucket

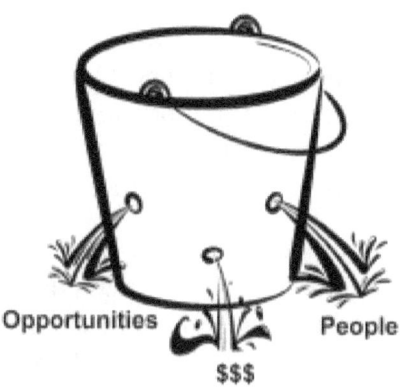

Being able to recognise and seize opportunities when they arise is how organisations exceed expectations and outshine their competitors. Calculated, confident and informed risk-taking leads to growth and innovation, but when the resilience bucket of your workplace is weak, those opportunities pass you by and in a blink of an eye you find yourself stagnated and stuck in survival mode. This leads to decreased margins, diminished brand equity and a declining net profit.

But the biggest loss that a weakened workplace bucket causes is the loss of great people. Attracting and retaining the best people in your industry is impossible when you have not created an environment where they can thrive. And therefore, when people and teams are not resilient, any bump in the road can turn into a major crisis because everyone's shock absorbers - their coping ability - have worn away.

Prioritising how you approach keeping the resilience buckets of your staff full will save you an enormous amount of time, stress, and money.

How To Strengthen A Workplace Bucket

There are many factors that can strengthen the workplace bucket but it is important to understand that due to each organisation being unique then the micro-changes must be relevant to their specific circumstances.

The first step is to implement policies and frameworks that create an environment where the people within the organisation have the ability to come to work and perform at their best. When this is done well it is often referred to as a thriving work culture.

The second step is to continually provide professional development programs – technical and non-technical - that educate and inspire everyone at all levels to be their best selves. My *Courageous Self-Leadership Masterclass,* which I mention in the upcoming chapter titled *Next Steps,* is a great example of one of these programs.

If we continue to use the examples of sleep, movement and nourishment, but this time at a workplace level, this is what could be considered:

1. **Sleep** - do you expect your team members to reply to emails or answer calls late at night? Does this prevent them from getting a reasonable amount of sleep so they can perform at their best the next day? France was the first country in the world to create a law that prevents employers who have more than fifty employees from contacting their people after hours. The goal is to protect private time and prevent their most valued asset – their people - from burning out.

2. **Movement** - are your team members required to work hours that are so long and intense that they cannot move their bodies, which we know will improve their physical health and cognitive ability?

3. **Nourishment** - do you supply soggy pastries and nutrient-deficient food during team meetings and/or events? What do you provide so your team members have the ability to make educated, nutritional decisions?

Other workplace bucket fillers could be flexible work arrangements, an investment in continued education, and/or effective workplace wellness programs.

It often only takes micro-changes in a workplace for big impacts to be experienced.

If you can create workspaces, frameworks, and education programs that ensure the resilience buckets of your people are kept close to full, the whole culture of your workplace will improve ... as will the bottom line.

Optimistic, resilient, healthy people make impactful, profitable businesses. It's as simple as that.

Self-leaders must take responsibility for looking after their own buckets, because when a self-leader's bucket is full, they are on fire. They are motivating, inspiring and can take on the world. But when a self-leader's bucket is depleted, then life can quickly unravel for themselves, for their teams and/or for the businesses they own or work in.

I invite you now to read on to this next chapter where I discuss how my self-leadership story of adversity has been turned into a self-leadership story of resilience, despite my bucket being stripped bare of all its resources.

Chapter Ten

Rage into RESILIENCE

"I can be changed by what happens to me. But I refuse to be reduced by it."

Maya Angelou

This brings me to the chapter that triggered the writing of this book in the first place.

I have procrastinated a lot about getting these next words to paper, and as I do it, a whole range of emotions come up. I am again questioning whether I should write about it, but I know deep down that if I want anything positive to come from the following horrible experience, then I need to complete this chapter, this book, and this story.

I need to extract the lessons I have learnt so I can complete my own healing, but I also want to extract a message and a truth about how we can all learn and forgive and rise up after adversity.

I want to turn my story of rage into a story of resilience.

Those close to me have said that my ability to get through this experience has solidified their belief in my resilience, strength and self-leadership, but I have to believe this about myself to be able to move forward.

> *"I've been cheered by thousands, booed by thousands, but nothing feels as bad as the booing inside your own head during those ten minutes before you fall asleep."*
> Andre Agassi

I have to be confident that I really have drawn insights from the decisions that I made and the actions that I took. I need to extract these lessons so that I can do better next time, and grow professionally and personally.

So here I go.

I was in a deep sleep in my room on the island of Tanna in Vanuatu, when I was woken from a loud noise. This noise, I later found out, was a petrol bomb that had been thrown at my bedroom.

In other countries they call them Molotov Cocktails, a crude weapon, which consists of a glass bottle semi-filled with flammable liquid and a cloth rag fixed securely around the mouth. The rag is lit prior to throwing the bottle, and once it hits its target and smashes, the burning rag causes the flammable liquid to explode.

As I came out of my sleep I could hear a dog barking, I could smell smoke and as soon as I opened my eyes, my whole body went into full alert, as I knew something was terribly wrong. My room had smoke in it and as I jumped up to see what was going on, I saw the terrifying sight of ferocious flames right outside my window.

When I looked out I could see that the car below my window was on fire, the whole building that I was in was on fire, as was the restaurant/bar area, the maintenance shed, and another bungalow, and there was a group of men silently, suspiciously running away, holding sticks of fire. They were not drunk and yahooing. They were being as quiet as they could be so we weren't alerted to the evil act they had just committed.

As I ran down the stairs and outside I couldn't believe what I was seeing. This beautiful little corner of the world that had been my second home for years was under attack by men who were so bent on an unwarranted revenge that they were willing to burn us alive while we slept to make their message heard.

You see, tragically a lovely local boy had been murdered three weeks before. This was a terrible shock to everyone as Vanuatu is known for its friendly, peaceful community life and murder is far from a usual occurrence. Unfortunately though, Ned, the son of the owner Hugh, of Tanna Lodge, where we were staying, had been accused of this murder.

Tanna Lodge had been great supporters of the work *Jump Start Foundation* had been doing for years and gave us free accommodation so we had more money for our literacy projects. I knew Hugh, Ned, and the family very well, and I also knew that there was no way that Ned would do anything like that. He was a kind-hearted, jovial young man who bent over backwards to help us in whatever way he could when we were on Tanna.

Sadly, Ned ended up spending seven long months in jail before his case was heard. Once the case was finally brought to court, the judge made an unequivocal decision that there was no case to answer to and made it very clear that there had never been sufficient evidence to arrest Ned in the first place. He was immediately released with an apology.

It's important for me to tell you this now so you can see how all of the pain and suffering that was coming our way, was all for nothing.

That night on Tanna, as I ran in terror from the burning building, I banged on Hugh's bedroom door and he came out screaming for me to evacuate everyone. It was just after midnight and of course, everyone was tucked away soundly in their bungalows with no idea of the nightmare that was unfolding.

Firstly, I ran to where I knew the co-director of my foundation was sleeping so she could start evacuating people on her side of the resort. As she came out, the men hurled rocks at her, damaging her neck and face, and breaking a bone in her hand. She was sixty-four years of age and five foot nothing. Hardly a threat to them, but of course, those men cared nothing about anyone.

I ran around, bashing on doors, screaming to my volunteers, as well as the half dozen other tourists staying at the resort, to quickly get dressed and move down to the beach away from the burning buildings. People were shrieking in horror as they ran from the engulfing flames while dodging the balls of fire that were falling from the burning roofs, and desperately looking out for the group of men who were hell-bent on harming us.

Apparently, when I woke two of our volunteers, they said that when they asked me what was going on, I said, *"The mongrels are back."* Because, you see, that afternoon there had been some trouble.

We had had the most wonderful day at Isangel Central Primary School, which was the school we had supported for years and where we had built the library that had been destroyed by Cyclone Pam. We spent the day clearing weeds from the gardens, scraping old paint from walls, re-cataloguing the new library books we had brought with us, playing games, reading stories, and exchanging a deep, mutual respect for the two communities who were working together to create education opportunities for the children.

We really had had a wonderful day, and for all the volunteers who had never been to Tanna or to our school before, they could not believe what they had experienced. It was the first volunteer trip that I had led where I did not know the majority of the participants, but one thing I knew from day one was that this group of women were motivating, inspiring, generous, smart, and kind beyond words. The work they had all done leading up to the trip to raise money, to buy stationery, to purchase new books, and to help in any way they could was incredible. The amount of gratitude I had towards these amazing volunteers before our plane had even touched down was pretty high.

When we arrived back to Tanna Lodge that first afternoon, full of hopes and plans for what the remainder of the week would bring and what we felt we could all accomplish, Hugh immediately came to tell me that they had had some strife during the day. A bunch of men from the top village, plus a large group of onlookers, had come down making a scene, aggressively forcing into their vehicles some of the local staff who had worked at Tanna Lodge for years, and threatening everyone else with a lot of trouble.

I immediately started to shake. What the hell was all this about? What had brought it on? Why now?

I called Daniel, one of the community leaders who had also been the principal of the school we supported, as he had been guiding me over the last few weeks about the on-the-ground situation since the tragic death of the local boy, and he had promised me that everything was safe and fine and I trusted him on that.

That afternoon, I asked him to explain to me why these men would be doing this when Ned had been charged (incorrectly) and put in jail, and the police were in the middle of investigating it all? It made no sense to me. Why were they causing this trouble for us?

He was adamant that I should not worry because it had now all been discussed and sorted out. I asked him over and over again if he was sure of this, and he kept saying, *"Yes, I am absolutely sure."*

No matter what he said though, I was still really worried because I knew there was nowhere else for us to go. SInce Cyclone Pam's carnage, all the accommodation had been destroyed or it was uninhabitable, and I also knew that the last plane had already left the island on that day. We were stuck no matter what was happening, as there were no alternatives for us to go anywhere else.

Another one of the village elders, Jeffrey, came down to talk to me about what had transpired. I have known Jeffrey for years and he is a very smart man who is fair and just and has always been an influential elder in that whole section of the island. He told me that local custom suggests that the people "related" to the deceased should not work for one month. They felt that due to Ned being (at that stage) accused of the murder, Tanna Lodge should be closed and should not be earning money. The local staff that had worked there for years should also stay home and grieve for the young man who had died, despite them needing to financially support their families.

I did not know prior to arriving that this was going to be an issue. I had spoken to umpteen leaders within the community after the young man's sad death about whether it was okay for us to come. They had all said without hesitation that there was absolutely no issue with us continuing our plans to come and support the community, because since the cyclone they needed all the help they could get. What we were now told though was that in the minds of these men, us being there during this time of mourning was disrespectful.

Despite the fact that we were only there to help their community to get back on their feet.

Despite the fact that for the last six months we had been busting our guts to raise enough money to feed their brothers, sisters, daughters, and cousins since Cyclone Pam had come through and destroyed their food supply.

Despite the fact that the water tank we had gifted the community plus the extra water tank that was on its way was a lifeline for hundreds of families in the area.

Despite the fact that all of our volunteers had taken time out of their lives to come and do whatever they could for this community.

Despite the fact that we had nothing to do with the terrible tragedy of the local boy who lost his life, and plus all our arrangements had been made months prior.

We understood that the family and the friends were grieving, and we had always had a deep respect for local customs, but we would have also liked to have some respect for what we were doing, or to be originally told to stay away.

Jeffrey told me that he had had a meeting and a cup of kava with these men in the nakamal because this is how they talk things through on Tanna. He reminded them that we were there to help repair the varying layers of physical and emotional damage that Cyclone Pam had caused their community and that they needed to put aside their issues surrounding Ned and his family and the staff while we were there.

Those men made a promise in front of their custom leaders (who often have far more "weight" than the local police) to set their grievances aside for the whole week while we were there volunteering, and then after we left on the Saturday it was agreed that they would continue their "discussions." If only they had kept their promise.

By this stage it was dark, and all our volunteers were in the dining room, laughing and eating and drinking and having a wonderful time talking about all that had gone on that day at the school and how excited they were for the next day's activities.

What should I do?

The two New Zealand police officers that had been mentoring the local police for the last eighteen months also came to talk to me. We had met them the night before and exchanged stories and a mutual respect for the work we were all doing on Tanna.

I suppose they alleviated my greatest fear, which was that these men would come back while we slept. Was that a premonition? Intuition? Why didn't I listen to my gut? Not that I could have done anything about it because we had nowhere to go, but perhaps we could have been more prepared.

The Kiwi police officers, though, convinced me that that would never happen. Man-Tanna (as they are referred to in Vanuatu) believe they have every justification to protest and show their anger and shout their injustices, because they believe they are right and want everyone to see and hear them. They would never come in the night because no one would be around to watch their performances.

I believed them, and after two hours of tears and trepidation, I went in to join my group.

It was here that I made a mistake. I decided not to tell anyone what had gone on.

I have gone over and over and over the conversations I had with the NZ police, the village elder, the principal, Hugh, with all of them, since that horrible night, wondering if I missed something that they had told me that would indicate we weren't safe.

I have also questioned myself a billion times as to my decision not to tell our group all about what had been transpiring. As far as they knew, everything was completely fine.

At the time, I made that decision because they had all convinced me that things were now okay, and especially after what the New Zealand policeman had told me about the men of Tanna only doing things in the daytime when everyone could see them doing it, I truly thought we would be all right. My thought process was to get a grasp of everything the following day, and if I felt that there was any whiff of further issues, then we would discuss it and make a decision together as to what to do.

Retrospect is a great thing and I know now that I should have been totally transparent with everyone. I still beat myself up that I wasn't, but I truly thought it was all going to be fine and I didn't want anyone to worry themselves unnecessarily. As their leader, worrying about all the bits and bobs in the background was my job.

When I later explained this to our volunteers, they were very quick to tell me that they understood why I had made that decision. It took much longer for me to forgive myself for it though ☹

It's still hard to comprehend why it all happened. Those men knew that Tanna Lodge had guests, and those men knew that we (*Jump Start Foundation*) were amongst the guests and we had been a welcome partner in their community for so so long. Their elders had spoken to them, and they had promised to leave us alone so we could complete our volunteer work. To then choose to come silently in the middle of the night to set us on fire while we were sleeping is malicious, and evil, and around the world this is considered nothing short of intentional homicide.

We evacuated everyone down to the beach, which was about forty metres from where everything was burning. It was pitch black and very cold and we didn't know where our attackers were, and of course there was no triple zero phone number to call for help on this isolated island. We were all petrified.

I remember not seeing "little Lily" who was here with her mum, Andrea, from the USA. They had seen all our good work online post-Cyclone Pam, and therefore made changes to their holiday plans so they could come and volunteer with us. Lily was only eight years of age and when I couldn't see her I immediately worried. I found Andrea and calmly asked her where Lily was and she said she was with "big Lily" – you see we had two Lily's with us, one was eight and the other one was sixteen.

I said to Andrea that I needed her to keep little Lily by her side at all times, so that when I saw her, I could also see her little one. We needed to keep everyone safe, and I needed to be able to know that little Lily was not out of our sight, especially since it was so dark and we had no idea where those men were and what they would do next.

We were worried that the tide was coming in and pushing us back towards the fires. The only place we could take refuge where it would be safer and drier was at some neighbouring huts. We trekked across the small creek and up the hill until we arrived at our destination for the long and scary night ahead. We were offered protection in their huts but we were all too scared of getting trapped inside if those men came again and set fire to where we slept.

Thankfully, I had been able to get through to my friends in Port Vila via our emergency mobile phone (mine was destroyed in the fires) and they immediately contacted the Australian High Commission. Throughout the night, my friends Andy and Regina, as well as the Australian High Commission continually called us to check on the fragility of our situation. Although they weren't with us during the following frightening hours, to have them on the end of the phone provided a little bit of comfort.

There was twenty-three women and one man, and although we didn't know much about each other, we huddled together for dear life in confusion, fear and trepidation about what the next five hours would bring. It was a long, freezing-cold night that we shivered through on the damp grass as we waited for help. We were in an isolated corner of a remote island, the vehicles had been destroyed with petrol bombs, and the only other resort on the island was not answering our calls for help. Unbelievably, the local police took two hours to respond to messages from the Australian High Commission to come and keep us safe, and we were twice approached by a bunch of menacing men who carried sticks of fire. We were simply terrified.

During those five long hours of fear, my whole body was on full alert, petrified that this group of incredible humans would be harmed even more – physically and psychologically - under my watch. I'll never forget at about 4am as I was anxiously watching over everyone as they spooned each other trying desperately to keep warm, I felt such a deep sense of guilt and despair that I had (unintentionally) put them in this situation.

When dawn finally broke, and we made our way back to Tanna Lodge, we could not believe what we saw. The place was destroyed. Those men had shattered decades of blood, sweat and tears, and hundreds of thousands of dollars that Hugh and his staff had invested in the community. What remained of the resort was still smoking and the repercussions of the crime were as clear as day. The place had been ruined. Hugh's business had been ruined. And if our predictions were right, *Jump Start Foundation* had been ruined.

Later that morning, the Australian High Commission in Port Vila organised two small planes to come and evacuate us. They sent over one of their staff members with food and water as all our supplies had been destroyed, and then later that day the Vanuatu Army was sent to Tanna to restore calm and order.

As we waited amongst the burnt ruins for our flights off the island, those men sent a message down to say if Hugh didn't leave with us on the planes, they would start killing his staff members. Even as I write this now, three years later, I still cannot believe that this beautiful, peaceful corner of the world that was such a part of my life had turned into such a nightmare.

The full impact of that night would not hit me for a quite a while though, because at the time I had to stay strong and focused and make logical decisions to protect and keep everyone safe. Because that was my job. I was their leader. I hadn't slept all night and all I wanted to do was curl up into a ball and cry, but it was not the time for that. My personal unravelling would need to wait its turn. I needed to put everyone else first before I even contemplated the consequences that this would have on me physically, financially and emotionally.

As we flew away from the island, I remember looking out of that window to the beautiful tropical jungles, which were surrounded by incredible turquoise waters, whose people I had cherished for over ten years, knowing that everything I had worked towards was now ruined and I would most likely never come back again. My despair finally escaped from the pit of my tummy and I sobbed on that departing plane in a way I had never done so before.

Once I finally arrived home to the safe and loving arms of my husband, the implications of that night started to set in. I have to say though that I could never have anticipated the complete unravelling that was about to occur because it ended up being far worse than I could have ever imagined.

Physically, I had some temporary lung damage as we did not know how long I had been breathing in the burning petrol fumes from the bombed vehicle outside my bedroom window. I had also broken a bone in my foot as I ran around barefoot evacuating people. The whole incident seemed to have flared up other injuries in my body too, such as a whiplash from a four-car accident eighteen months previously, and a spinal fracture from twenty-two years ago. Weird.

There were also financial consequences because I could not work for a whole year. Part of this time was supposed to be my "sabbatical" after selling my business, but certainly not the whole time. And I certainly hadn't predicted that my "sabbatical" would involve such rage, despair, and a loss so deep I didn't know if I would ever feel purposeful again. The work I had been doing in Vanuatu for so many years filled me up, and now we would never be able to go back. I mean, how would I look a volunteer in the eyes and truthfully be able to tell them that Tanna was safe? I couldn't. And how would I look a potential employer in the eyes and truthfully be able to tell them that I would be a great choice for their company? I couldn't. This meant an extended period of time without a job and without an income.

But it was the emotional consequences that had the biggest impact. I suffered through twelve months of post-traumatic stress disorder, which involved nightmares, flashbacks, crippling insomnia, depression, suicidal thoughts, and a rage so powerful that it was destroying me.

I had to get my head around the fact that my life's purpose was no longer. I had not been able to have my own children, but I always felt that the universe had decided this so that I could dedicate my heart and soul to two hundred children in the south pacific. But now this was gone.

What I learnt about trauma during my therapy sessions is that there are four things that can hold your progress back:

1. **Sleep:** When you are awoken from a deep sleep, and are faced with a life or death situation as I was, then your body and brain unconsciously fears going to sleep. It wants to stay alert in case something else puts you in danger. This hyper vigilance makes it incredibly difficult to fall asleep. When you don't sleep, you don't heal. Insomnia can ruin you.

2. **Intentional harm:** If the trauma comes about due to intentional action this adds another layer to the healing process. Some trauma occurs by being "in the wrong place at the wrong time." This does not make it any less horrible, but when people set out to intentionally harm you, it takes you to places emotionally that you never thought you would be in.

3. **Justice:** So often, I have seen on TV victims and families talk about getting justice for what happened to them. I could see how important this would be, but never until this particular event did I fully understand how crucial it is to the recovery process. When bad people do bad things, you expect that our world is set up in a way that means they will be punished. The punishment is never enough that you feel it to be worthwhile, but it allows you to gain back a smidge of belief in a society that ensures that when bad things happen to good people, there are repercussions. The men who intentionally tried to burn us alive while we slept have never been brought to justice and that fuelled my rage for a long time.

4. **Betrayal:** When a trauma occurs and there is personal betrayal involved, healing is harder. The betrayal that occurred that night and in the months after affected me deeply.

    I felt betrayed by the community who I had helped for many years because they didn't "dob in" those men.

    I felt betrayed by the local police whose job it is to protect us, yet I found out they had actually suggested to these men that they set the fires for "payback."

I felt betrayed by the Vanuatu Government, whose deputy prime minister had emailed me promising they would punish all those involved, including the Tanna police. That never happened.

I felt betrayed by a teacher at the school where *Jump Start Foundation* had built the library who knew that those men were going to do what they did, but he chose not to warn us.

I felt betrayed by the Australian Embassy who told me that they would not be able to assist us to get justice because this would impact their relationship with the Vanuatu Government.

The final betrayal came from the management committee of my own foundation. I ended up having to make the extremely difficult decision to resign as President so I could look after my deteriorating wellbeing. It's probably the most heart-wrenching decision I have ever had to make. I thought that due to the fact that I had started this foundation by myself fourteen years before, that I would be given the opportunity to access my emails and documents that were important to me. Unfortunately though, the new committee did not trust in my professional capabilities anymore because of the PTSD and made a hardball decision to immediately cut off my access to everything. Before I could save all the beautiful emails of support that people had sent me after this terrible event, they shut down my email account, treated me like I was untrustworthy, and changed passwords to files that I believe belonged to me personally. When I was at my lowest, they stripped me bare.

I do understand that there are two sides to every story and I'll never really know why all these betrayals unfolded as they did. All I know is that they had a deep, negative impact on my life at a time when I needed all the support I could get.

One of the many post-traumatic stress disorder symptoms that I experienced because of all of this was that I started to catastrophise. This became quite a problem for me and one of these new illogical fears was of not being able to escape my bedroom if we had a fire at home. I'd never in my life worried about this but it started to consume me.

One day I decided that a solution to this fear would be to buy a big rope so I could tie it to my bed leg and this would allow me to climb out of our second-storey bedroom if there was a house fire. Surely I would feel better now knowing that I could escape if need be?

As I walked the aisles of the hardware shop looking for a rope that would hold my weight, I started to realise that this rope could also put me out of my own misery. What a relief this would be, not only to this unbearable life that I had been enduring due to so much loss, but also a relief for everyone around me who in my mind I had become such a miserable burden to. This was ten months after the incident but the repercussions of what happened had unravelled me to a point where I was now suicidal. I frightened myself that day, and knew I needed some intensive help to get over what I had been through.

There is no doubt, that that night changed me forever. Up until the writing of this book, I thought that the change was an awful change. I didn't like this new version of Heidi Dening. In fact, I was ashamed of what she had become – weak, scared, jittery, angry, gloomy, and with a 'poor-me' attitude. I felt pathetic.

Reflection

Thankfully though, I've finally been able to dig deep and draw out valuable lessons from that dreadful experience and I can now honestly say that it has become a positive turning point in my life. I now understand so much more about unsustainable loyalty, about trusting your gut, about responsibility and forgiveness, and mostly about resilience.

What experiences have you had to endure that have caused you so much rage in your life?

How have they influenced you?

What have you learnt from them?

How have you transformed that rage into resilience?

I learnt the following *Self-Leadership Strategies* about **RAGE** and **RESILIENCE** after that petrol bomb experience in Vanuatu.

1. Unsustainable Loyalty

To have built a not-for-profit from scratch and then to produce the incredible results that we did, when we had to scrape and beg for every dollar, and take no remuneration for it, was something to this day, I still feel proud of.

We had set ourselves a goal of creating life-changing opportunities by improving the levels of literacy, and there was nothing that was going to stop us from achieving that.

Unfortunately, even though I felt immense personal loyalty to the community that we had made this promise to, the model was unsustainable. The reality was that to continually achieve our goals I would need to make personal and professional sacrifices that would jeopardise my own health, my own relationships, my own future … and in the end, my own life.

My deep loyalty, which has always been an important value of mine, nearly killed me.

In a work situation, being loyal to a project, a person, a client, or a company when you know it is not right can have detrimental impacts on your physical, mental, professional and financial wellbeing.

Sometimes things that we start evolve into things we can't sustain. It takes courage to walk away from a dream. Recognising though how detrimental the pursuit of that dream is takes an enormous amount of honesty, self-reflection, and mental strength.

2. Trusting Your Gut

Listening to your gut feeling in all parts of your life is crucial. When you learn to pay attention to your intuition then you tap into a deep level of guidance that helps you make the right decisions.

This is hard when we live in this 24/7 society because it's really difficult to take the time, to clear a space, and to embrace the silence that is needed for these profound messages to be heard.

I'm going to go a bit "woo woo" now. Watch out.

For the few years before this life-changing incident, I had been struggling to sustain what was required to fulfil our promise.

The universe had started to send me messages, but I ignored them. My brain and body were telling me to slow down, stop putting the *Jump Start Foundation* projects before everything else, but I was so determined to complete what I started that I ignored every warning sign.

When Cyclone Pam destroyed everything we had accomplished, I should have trusted my gut and said, *"We cannot start this over. We did our best, we achieved it (even though it was only operating for eight months before being ruined), and now we need to let it go."*

I did not want to have to think about building that damn library again. The thought of it actually made me feel ill due to knowing the amount of work required and what this would take from my life.

But no, my unsustainable loyalty to this community was unshakeable and I chose deafness when every part of me was screaming that it was all too hard. People were telling me that "enough was enough", but I was too stubborn.

The universe had other ideas though. I didn't listen to the message it sent with the cyclone; I didn't listen when there was initial unrest after that poor local boy had been killed; I didn't listen when they came that day and forcefully removed staff; so the universe "upped the ante" and sent in petrol bombs.

"Now, Heidi," it screamed, *"will you start to listen?"*

Whether you believe this type of thing or not, it makes sense to trust your intuition.

Self-leaders know when their brain and body are talking to them. It takes time to translate this intuitive language, but once you grasp that alphabet, you wonder how you ever survived before.

Trusting in your gut in a workplace is one of the most courageous skills you can learn. Not everyone that surrounds you at work is willing to do the right thing by you. Office politics and toxic cultures are rife. Learning to tap into your intuition so you can thoughtfully make the right decisions based on what your gut is telling you takes vulnerability, self-awareness and courage.

This intuition skill is one of the most powerful skills that a self-leader can acquire.

3. Responsibility and Forgiveness

For quite a while I blamed myself for what had happened to us that night. I believed that if I had listened harder, asked better questions, not been so determined to help the school, then I would have heard different messages.

I never divulged to anyone that I was blaming myself. But when you are the leader, when everyone is looking to you to make the right decisions, then it is hard not to feel responsible when bad shit happens.

When you blame yourself though for something, it festers inside of you and makes you physically and mentally unwell and unable to heal.

Blame rots your resilience bucket from the inside out, and very soon big, gaping holes start to spill your resources until you are left with nothing.

You often see the consequences of blame in workplaces. People who don't take responsibility for their actions yet want to blame everyone else to cover their own tracks. A blame-centred work environment creates a toxic work culture. It rots the workplace bucket and very soon you see good opportunities, hard-earned dollars, and great staff seeping through the holes.

Taking ownership of your actions, especially when you fail, takes a huge amount of courage. To say, *"I stuffed up"* out loud to your friends, your family and your colleagues is hard, but the respect you gain after doing that is worth its weight in gold.

4. RESILIENCE

Resilience is defined when a person has the ability to:

- adjust to adversity;
- recover from life's setbacks; and
- move forward with their life in a positive manner.

There is no actual measuring tool for us to know how we are going or how we compare to others. It's all very subjective, but it is definitely a pretty hot topic right now because I am asked to address it a lot in my education workshops and keynote presentations.

People have told me I am resilient because of the unusual experiences that have occurred in my life and the fact that they haven't broken me. I think those men who intentionally tried to burn us alive, did break me for a while. BUT they did not break me forever.

Does that mean I lost some of my resilience along the way, or has it given me even more resilience now?

Who knows?

I do know, as I talked about in my last chapter, that my resilience bucket was running on empty before this event, so the chances of me not breaking were pretty slim.

Saying I have more resilience now than ever before is probably true. I really hope that it is not tested to its full extent for a while though. I would like some time off. I would like to move forward and be grateful and proud of who I am and what I have become. I don't want to be tested anymore ... well, not for a while anyway.

I had so much rage for what those men had done, and the consequences their actions had on my life and the lives of so many others. But I have to admit that a lot of that rage was also directed at myself. I believed that I had a part to play in that terrible incident because of my unsustainable loyalty and the fact that I did not listen to my own intuition.

This rage festered inside of me for three years to a point where it literally had started to rot my insides. You see, I had been suffering very bad pelvic pain and nausea for about ten months and had had every poo, wee, blood, and breath test available plus numerous scans to try and identify what was going on. Everything kept coming back as being completely healthy but I knew that something wasn't right. I mean, daily debilitating pain and nausea so bad that you can't look at food is not normal. A week before my decision to write this book, a specialist decided that I should have some investigative surgery to see what they could find. On that surgical table, they finally found the answer to what had been going on. I had adenomyosis and stage four endometriosis that was covering my uterus, ovaries, kidneys, bowel, rectum and appendix. My appendix was so bad they had to remove it.

My emotional rage had transformed into a physical disease that was damaging my insides and this made me realise that the time had come when I needed to forgive myself. My health is incredibly important to me and holding on to all that rage, blame and betrayal was rotting me from the inside out and putting my wellbeing in jeopardy. It had to stop.

When all that chaos was occurring in Vanuatu, I genuinely did do everything I thought was right. I was trying to be the best leader I could be. I wish I could turn back time and do things differently and make different decisions, but of course that is not possible. Instead, I want to learn from my experiences and be a better person and a better self-leader because of them.

I want to have the courage to finally turn this story of rage into a story of resilience.

Those men took a lot from my life but I am forever grateful that they did not take the lives they had hoped to take.

Has this incident given me more resilience? Who is to know? How is it measured anyway?

What I do know is that from all the stories I have shared with you, I have learnt so much. And that is all I can expect from myself. And that is all we can expect from each other.

More than anything, I want those who know me and love me to always think of me as someone who will bravely step up and speak out, and for them to say … *"See that girl over there? Her Middle Name Is Courage."*

Chapter Eleven

Phoenix
RISING

*"And just as the Phoenix rose from the ashes,
she too will rise.
Returning from the flames,
clothed in nothing but her strength,
more beautiful than ever before."*

Shannen Heartzs

In Greek mythology, a phoenix is a colourful and vibrant bird that is associated with the sun.

He or she arises from flames as a victor, beating all of life's challenges and overcoming hard times. Therefore, the phoenix represents renewal and the conquering of challenges, and is a symbol of rebirth from the ashes of the past.

I have been surprised how many people have told me that their image of me after the Vanuatu petrol bombs was of a phoenix rising. Even a mentor of mine suggested I complete my book with this chapter about the symbolic meaning of the phoenix and how it relates to my life.

I must admit that I really love the idea that those who know me see me this way.

And from now on, it is the way I will see myself.

I have come out of those flames (literally), and moved through the PTSD, the pain, the grief, the loss, the despair, and the rage, until I have become a more resilient and vibrant woman who is determined to turn that painful story into one of positivity.

I have always said that going to Vanuatu was a "sliding door" moment for me, and I truly believe my life would have taken a completely different and less fulfilling path if it were not for that first life-changing opportunity as a twenty-year-old. Since then, many of my favourite personal experiences during my lifetime have occurred over there.

Memories include running through bougainvillea-lined villages while "high-fiving" the kids; scuba diving and snorkelling some of the best coral reefs in the world; handing over more than two tonnes of literacy packs to children who deserve equal educational opportunities; romantic dinners under the stars; drinking cocktails out of coconuts;

reading stories to eager, smiling children; doing the South Pacific's largest and most enthusiastic version of the hokey pokey; dancing the heel-and-toe-polka; walking on the rim of an active volcano; catching a seven-foot marlin; empowering teenage girls through workshops and sport; seeing the pride in my parents' eyes when they came with me to share what I had done; working alongside the Australian Defence Force and New Caledonia Military after Cyclone Pam; winning awards; and most of all, building the library at Isangel Central Primary School. The official opening will remain one of the proudest days of my life.

I now remember all this joy.

I now remember how positive my experiences were.

I now remember how it shaped my life into one that I am proud of.

I now remember all the good I did and the life-changing opportunities through literacy that I provided to hundreds and hundreds of children.

I will not let one evil act delete all the goodness that came from the years I spent there.

Every learning I have extracted from each of the stories in this book has strengthened my resilience bucket and now that vessel is as hard as steel.

I have conquered challenges.

I have renewed.

I have risen.

Because that is who I am.

I am the Phoenix.

I am Heidi Dening.

AND MY MIDDLE NAME IS COURAGE!

About The Author

"If It's Going To Be It's Up To Me"

My Mission

I hate seeing people not living their life to the fullest. That is why I have a mission to educate and inspire as many self-leaders as I can on how they can continue to strengthen their resilience buckets so they can step up, speak out and share their brilliance with the world. I believe that this will then send a ripple effect of vitality, resilience and optimism into our workplaces, into our families, and into our communities ... potentially improving the lives of hundreds of thousands of people.

My Professional Life

Despite what that careers advisor told me when I was fifteen, I've actually gone from being a plump, pimply, painful teenager to a sought-after keynote speaker, an award-winning business owner, a global advisor for workplace mental health, and a passionate educator who believes that authentic, resilient and gutsy self-leaders will make the biggest difference to our world.

My long-term passion and commitment to education and vitality for all walks of society - from corporate professionals, to small business owners, to entrepreneurs, and children living on remote islands of Vanuatu - has meant I have received many awards that I am extremely proud of. These various awards include an Australia Day Merit Award,

Westpac's International Women's Day Local Hero Award, and I was included on the honour roll for the global #CelebratingWomen project. Who would have thought?

To add to this growing list of achievements that I really didn't think was possible all those years ago, I have become a global advisor regarding workplace mental health with the International WELL™ Building Institute.

Oh, and last but not least, an author of a self-leadership book. Far out ☺

My Personal Life

I am incredibly grateful to be living in one of Sydney's most scenic and historic suburbs with my gorgeous husband, Ken, and our three rescue fur-babies. A dog called Lady Beetle, and two kitty-kats called Daisy Flower and Dimples. I ADORE them all. We have extraordinary neighbours and I never thought it would be possible to have such a country town experience while living in one of the world's best cities.

Growing up, I was a passionate and moderately talented tennis player, hitting thousands of balls with my Dad on our backyard tennis court and competing in tournaments around the State. My body is old now, and won't tolerate my physical gusto for playing, so I am a dedicated spectator who instead enthusiastically follows grand slam tournaments in person and from the couch. I've been to Wimbledon twice with my parents, to the Australian Open twenty times with my girlfriends, and best of all I got to see my favourite, Rafa, win at Roland Garros. Woohoo.

There's no denying, I've always prioritised good health because I know how much more you get from life when you feel physically and mentally strong. I love to exercise and try to nourish my body with fresh, wholesome food every day, but without guilt or shame, I save all my naughty calories for good wine. Buttery chardonnays might be out-of-fashion but that does not stop me from enjoying a glass … or three.

About The Author

Lastly, I have an obsession with pretty dresses and can be easily talked into complementing them with matching handbags and shoes ... much to my husband's (and our bank account's) distress. ☺

That's me in a nutshell.

Thanks so much for reading.

Yours Courageously,

Heidi Jane x

Next Steps

*Courage isn't having the strength to go on –
it is going on when you don't have the strength."*

Napoleon Bonaparte

I'm sure you will now agree, that it is the courageous self-leaders of this world who are making a real difference. It took me many years to develop and get my own personal results from the strategies that you have read about in this book, but now that I've extracted the 'gold' I want to continue to share how to achieve those transformations.

Let's keep this conversation alive so we can all reap the benefits from increasing the number of authentic, resilient, and gutsy self-leaders around the globe.

To gain access to the following resources and services, please visit www.HeidiDening.com

Resilience Bucket – *A FREE 2min Quiz*

You now know that being a courageous self-leader is difficult when your bucket is depleted of its resources. To find out how full your resilience bucket is, take the quiz.

Masterclass - *Courageous Self-Leadership*

If you love the concepts of this book and believe that your work colleagues would thrive from understanding these self-leadership strategies, visit my website for more information.

Keynote Presentation - *Her Middle Name Is Courage*

If you would benefit from an experienced self-leader delivering a motivating keynote presentation at your next event, reach out to me via the website.

Can We Connect More?

I would love to get to know more about who you are and how you are planning to sprinkle your courageous self-leadership around the world. Let's start a conversation together via one (or all!) of these social networks:

in /HeidiDening

f /HeidiDeningSelfLeader

◉ /HeidiDening

🌐 /www.HeidiDening.com

If you like communicating in the old fashion (but highly personal) way, you can write to me at:

PO Box 635,
Balmain,
NSW, 2041

Sydney, Australia

Gratitude

*"Gratitude unlocks the fullness of life
and turns what we have into enough.
It can turn a meal into a feast, a house into a home,
a stranger into a friend."*

Melody Beattie

It has taken a huge amount of courage to write this book. To put one's own stories, deepest fears, greatest failings, and most impactful lessons into words for everyone to read, entails vaults of vulnerability mixed with a barrel of bravery.

But it also requires the efforts, support, encouragement and patience of a whole team of people in the background.

I'd firstly like to thank my beautiful Mum, Helen Dening, and my superhero Dad, Barry Dening, for laying the foundations of my courageous self-leadership from such an early age. Whatever I dreamed of doing, they encouraged me to strive for it, knowing that if I failed they would be there to pick up the pieces. No matter how often or how deeply I botched things up, they were always there to love me, reassure me and gently persuade me to keep on trying.

To my incredible sister, Katryna, who has been by my side through my best days and my worst. We have gone through so much together, but no matter what, she has been that caring, intelligent, thoughtful friend who always has my best interests at heart… even when those interests have been a little crazy. Her feedback and editing of this book were essential ... as is her presence in my life.

I must also thank Jenine L for her generous and honest feedback throughout the process. What a difference a talented wordsmith can make. A callout to Duncan F for encouraging me to delete one hundred and fifty two exclamations marks, to Suzi D for her brilliant marketing expertise, and to Jade P for her reassurance and fine-tuning during that last edit.

During the year that I hit rock bottom after nearly being burnt alive in Vanuatu, there were some very special people whose love and small acts of kindness during this terrible time helped me to put myself back together again. Thank you Anny P, Chris M, David S, Emma R, Hugh L, Julie D, Katryna D, Ken D, Kylie H, Lesley P, Lisa C, Naysan F, Magdaleen K, Marni P, Melissa L, Siobhan K and Yvonne P. You probably don't even remember your thoughtful gestures, but I do, and my memory is long. Thank you.

After that event, I thought I would never be able to regain my ability in public speaking because I had become such a nervous-nelly. I would like to thank everyone at my local Toastmasters Club in Balmain, Sydney for creating an environment that allowed me to take baby steps back to being a speaker. An extra special thanks goes to Allan for his gentle encouragement from day one.

To all the gals in my HerBusiness Marketing Mastermind group. When I told you about my idea to create a book and a keynote presentation called *Her Middle Name Is Courage* and why I felt the need to do this, your immediate positive comments were incredibly motivating. In fact, you really gave me the last piece of courage I needed to make this happen. Thank you.

A big thank you goes to Dave T and all his crew at the Inspirational Book Writers Retreat – AJ McC, Heather B, and Davina D. The space, care, reassurance and support that you provided on Stradbroke Island as I wrestled with demons to bring this book to life will never be forgotten. An extra big thanks to AJ for capturing the essence of the Phoenix Rising for my front cover photo.

Lastly, to the best leprechaun in the whole world. You have believed in me and boosted my courage every single day of our marriage and words cannot describe the gratitude I have for our life together. That night when we first met when you were king kong and I was bat girl still remains the luckiest day of my life.

I could never have written this book without you. Firstly, you encouraged me to stretch myself beyond what I thought I was capable of by going to Stradbroke Island with other 'real' book writers. You then proudly told everyone who would listen that your wife was on an island writing her book. But most importantly, you read and re-read all my chapters and helped me turn my point form stories that I didn't deem worthy of a book, into stories of colour and texture so that people would want to read them.

Your unshakeable belief that I am destined for great heights fills every single cell of mine with gratitude. I truly cannot believe that I am so loved by someone as remarkable as you. Thank you blue eyes x

Praise for Heidi Dening

One of the Best Speakers I Have Worked With – Selling Out In 24hrs

"I have had the pleasure of working with Heidi after engaging her to speak at a breakfast event on International Women's Day. Heidi is without doubt one of the best speakers I have worked with, ensuring that her presentation was tailored to fit the needs of the audience and our business. Her ability to engage the audience and create an interactive atmosphere to facilitate open discussion and sharing is outstanding. Heidi's talk attracted the most attendees to our breakfast session to date, selling out within the first 24hrs of release. I would highly recommend Heidi to speak at an event, or run a workshop directly with your team. In addition to the quality of her content, she is also just great and easy to work with."

Sarah Ferraina
Marketing and Communications Leader, Beaumont People

She Brought Great Energy, Warmth and Insight

"Heidi did a fantastic job emceeing the ASBAQ conference, and brought great energy, warmth and insight to the conference."

Mark McCrindle
Social Researcher and Demographer

Heidi is Authentic, Inspirational and Provides Useful Leadership and Burnout Prevention Tips

"We had the pleasure of Heidi Dening speaking at our Sydney, Melbourne, Adelaide and Perth conferences this year, which was themed 'Making a Difference'. Heidi truly made a difference with the audiences. She is professional, always prepared and easy to work with. Heidi is authentic, inspirational and provides the audience with useful leadership and burnout-prevention tips that they can use in their everyday life and at work. The online personal wellness audit that she provided for our delegates meant that they were engaged with our event before it even started, were encouraged to implement micro-changes from what they learnt, and they could then track their improvements after they went home. Feedback from our surveys was excellent and I would highly recommend Heidi for Speaker sessions or group training within your organisation."

Judith Beck
CEO, Financial Executive Women

Her Enthusiasm and Love of What She Does Shone Through

"The Association of Business Administrators (Qld) Inc engaged Heidi to be the emcee for our State Conference. We were looking for someone who could bring something completely different to the MC role in that we wanted, yes, an MC, but also someone who could expand on this role and add extra value for the delegates attending. Heidi's enthusiasm and love of what she does shone through over the three days and the way in which she shared her knowledge was well received by all those present. I totally look forward to hearing her present again somewhere in the future."

Kym Schultz
Conference Chair, ASBAQ 18

Heidi Exceeded my High Expectations

"As Australia's longest established conference organiser, I must have seen thousands of presentations from skilled professionals but Heidi exceeded the high expectations that I had by being an engaging, inspiring and informative speaker. Her brain and body rejuvenation sessions were simply amazing and gratefully appreciated by all."

Bryan Holliday
Chairman, ICMSA (International Conferences Management Services Australasia)

Simple Behavioural Changes to Prevent Team Burnout

"Heidi delivered an excellent session with my busy project team. Her enthusiastic and positive style kept everyone engaged in the difficult after lunch session, but more importantly, her pragmatic and accessible message meant that the team took action after the session and were able to enact simple behavioural changes to be healthier and happier. In a high pressure, high workload environment this was gold for me, taking action to prevent the team from burning out."

Frieda Maher
Owner, Sales Performance on Demand

Knowledge, Delivery, Personality and Enthusiasm

"I had the pleasure of speaking recently at a Leadership Summit where Heidi was also a speaker. The energy she immediately brought to the room was captivating. I was particularly impressed with her ability to have such a profound impact with her Brain and Body rejuvenation session - amazing how much of a difference she could make to me and the audience in such a short time frame. Heidi certainly stands out in terms of her knowledge, delivery, personality and enthusiasm for an area where she has passion.

Ronnie Altit
CEO and Founder, Insentra

The Feedback We Received was Unanimously Positive

"Heidi deserves her reputation, as she slotted in seamlessly with our line-up of speakers (senior executives and leaders from AT&T and Westpac, for example) at the Company Culture & Disruptive Leadership Summit. I would recommend Heidi to not only engage and inspire an audience, but get them to think differently."

Julie Alexander
Executive Director, Changing Change International

You Could Hear A Pin Drop

"There is no doubt that you are a true professional in your business. The talk kept everyone interested throughout and you could hear a pin drop throughout your presentation. Question time really indicated just how much of an interest it was."

David Firth
General Manager, Enfield NSW Pak Pacific Corporation plant, a division of AMCOR Ltd.

Transforming Audiences in All Industries

"We have utilised Heidi's excellent skills as a motivational speaker, menu consultant and conference emcee. Heidi's ethos is to transform habits long-term and in this regard her messages are real and meaningful. More importantly, they apply to all sectors and can be easily applied to all skill sets. Heidi provides thought-provoking and well-researched data for each client and I would have no hesitation in recommending her services."

Emma Bowyer
Managing Director, ICMSA
(International Conferences Management Services Australasia)

Her Wisdom, Knowledge and Energy was Outstanding

"I was an attendee at an immersive culture change summit where Heidi Dening was a speaker. Her wisdom, knowledge and energy was really quite outstanding. What I hadn't anticipated learning was the detrimental impact that an unhealthy culture has to an organisation and to the performance of the employees."

Warren Bingham
Executive Chairman, MedTech International

Strategies That Have Made a Big Difference to My Life

"Heidi has an exceptional skill of instilling in everyone an emotional strength and a very strong belief that anything is possible for those who wish to apply themselves. As a professional in the finance industry, often travelling for work, and leading a very hectic lifestyle, having endurance in the workplace is very important to me, (i.e. fit body, fit mind). This level of motivation and belief is something that you cannot buy, and I am fortunate to have been a recipient of this, and have now been able to apply it to many parts of my life. The level of dedication Heidi gives is extraordinary, and her passion for business is very evident."

Linda Stangherlin
Financial Industry Leader

Notes

www.ingramcontent.com/pod-product-compliance
Lightning Source LLC
Chambersburg PA
CBHW021407210526
45463CB00001B/252